WHY WE

Tara Scully

edited by Bridget G. Wendling

EAT FOOD

Kendall Hunt
publishing company

Cover image © Shutterstock, Inc.

Kendall Hunt
publishing company

www.kendallhunt.com
Send all inquiries to:
4050 Westmark Drive
Dubuque, IA 52004-1840

Copyright © 2016 by Kendall Hunt Publishing Company.

ISBN 978-1-4652-9875-1

Printed in the United States of America

Table of Contents

Section 1   **WHY WE AREN'T ALONE**   **1**

A Look at Ecology and Species Interactions   1

Basic Interactions Between Organisms   5

Trophism: Who Eats Whom (and What Do They Get Out of It)   6

Get the Skinny   10

Section 2   **WHO IS THAT IN MY CHEESE PUFFS?**   **13**

The Organisms That Are Our Food   13

Get the Skinny   24

Section 3   **WHERE ARE THOSE TRANS FATS?**   **27**

What We Get From Other Organisms   27

Get the Skinny   40

Section 4   **HOW DOES YOUR FOOD GET FROM YOUR MOUTH TO YOUR DERRIERE?**   **43**

Food Production, Enzymes and Reactions, and Digestion   43

Food Production   43

Enzymes and Reactions   46

Enzymatic Reactions   48

Digestion   49

Get the Skinny   54

Section 5   **YOU'RE GOING TO PUT THAT IN THERE?**   **57**

Moving and Storing Nutrients   57

Get the Skinny   64

Section 6   **WHAT'S THE DEAL WITH ENERGY DRINKS?**   **67**

Energy Production and Your Metabolism   67

Get the Skinny   79

Section 7   **WHEN IS FOOD NOT YOUR FRIEND?**   **81**

Health-Related Food Issues   81

Body Image and Eating Disorders   88

Get the Skinny   91

Section 1
WHY WE AREN'T ALONE

A Look at Ecology and Species Interactions

FOOD FOR THOUGHT

Your body is an ecosystem, and as a human, you need other organisms to survive. Because all the food you consume contains other organisms or compounds created from other organisms, you need to know how they can impact your body. And that is what this text is about.

Why do you eat food? How does it affect your body? These are two questions you should consider daily. In today's world, people often consume things without thinking about the impact of their actions. Sometimes it's a matter of convenience, other times it's a matter of ignorance or just habit. Maybe you are disconnected from the origin of your food and don't even consider why you are eating it. One goal of this course is to get you to think about why you eat the food you do. If you understand more clearly the connection between your body and the things you consume, you will be more likely to make healthier choices.

There is a barrage of information about nutrition and health—from infomercials, product advertisements, labeling on food, and even guidelines from the government—that is confusing, contradictory, and some-times misleading. If you understand, even on a very basic level, what happens when you consume things, you will not be misled; you will be able to discern the meaning of a food label; and ultimately, you will be equipped to be healthier.

If you grasp and retain the information set forth in this text, you will see on a daily basis how it applies to your body, your state of mind, and your overall well-being. You likely will find yourself (already an edu-cated individual) learning a lot about what is in the food you eat and how challenging it can be for a less educated person to eat well. Obesity, chronic disease, and several preventable diseases can be directly correlated to economic factors and lack of education on health issues. A goal of this text is to help you understand how to adopt sustainable, scientifically valid habits for good health. If each of us adopts a more mindful approach to eating, we can reduce the instances of obesity and impact our communities in far-reaching ways.

Additionally, it is essential that you are connected to your food. What does this mean? You need to understand where your food comes from; why it matters where you purchase it; why it matters how it was raised; what happens after you eat it; and what impact your consumption of it has on the world around you.

THE HUMAN BODY AS AN ECOSYSTEM

The human body is a complex and fascinating scientific wonder. Its systems and functions have been studied and analyzed extensively, and our understanding of its abilities and requirements is continuously evolving. If you understand your body and its relationship to food and nutrition, you can enhance your time on this planet by learning some essential skills:

- How to make better food choices;
- How to eat to feel better;
- How to manage a healthy weight;
- How nutrition affects your muscles, skin, digestive tract, and metabolism;
- How to protect your body from some diseases;
- How to help your body function more efficiently;
- What food is essential fuel for your body and what should be avoided; and
- How disease is generally an accumulating effect of repeatedly eating poorly or without regard to its impact on your health.

To do these things, you need to understand how your body uses food. First, however, you must get a general understanding of some scientific information that will be relevant to your greater understanding of this topic. For example, simply having a basic understanding of ecosystems is essential so that you can begin to understand not only your body's relationship with food and nutrition, but also your body's role in the world. If you think of your body as an ecosystem, and not merely as "yours," you can gain a greater appreciation of its impact and role. Additionally, a basic grasp of what defines "life" is essential so that you can grasp several concepts throughout the course. In short, we will only explore in depth some very basic (yet complex!) biology concepts in order to provide you with a general understanding so that you can relate it to food and your body.

You're welcome.

WHAT IS AN ECOSYSTEM?

An **ecosystem** is a defined space plus the nonliving (**abiotic**) and living (**biotic**) factors in that space. The living and nonliving components in this community interact and are dependent upon one another on various levels.

Scientists study ecosystems to learn from their cycles of input and output. Examples of ecosystems include tropical forests, ponds, deserts, and, as you will hopefully come to appreciate, the human body. The human body is actually composed of many ecosystems—for example, your skin, nose, blood, and most obviously, your digestive tract. Think of your body as being a synergy of multiple ecosystems that require one another; this holistic approach will enable you to see how all the various systems in your body are actually components of one larger ecosystem. Your body's ecosystem requires interaction with other ecosystems to acquire essential **nutrients** (such as food and minerals), and all of the ingredients to make the larger substances (such as proteins and carbohydrates) that allow us to function and thrive by enabling us to manufacture new cells.

 BOIL IT DOWN 1.1 If you are interested in discovering more information about the differences between atoms, search subatomic particles.

Whether we are describing nonliving or living factors, all substances in the universe are made up of combinations of the same components that come in different varieties; these are called **elements**. There are 92 naturally occurring elements, which are substances that have unique physical and chemical properties.

Structurally, elements are atoms that can be combined together and allow the resulting substances to have different properties. To understand why we eat food, we do not need to delve into the intricacies of **atoms** (units of elements made up of a specific combination of materials), **elements** (physically and chemically unique substances due to the amount and materials present), and **molecules** (combination of atoms from elements), you can explore these complex topics by doing the **BOIL IT DOWN** activities.

 CHEW ON THIS 1.1 Microelements are the nutrients you require in small quantities. Macroelements are the nutrients you require in large quantities. Ninety-six percent of your body weight is made up of just four macroelements, while less than 4% is made up of seven specific microelements and the remaining 1% is made up of trace elements.

ABIOTIC = NON-LIVING

As we said, **abiotic** factors in your body's ecosystem are the non-living things with which you interact. Some major ones include things you interact with literally every second and every day of your life, such as water, gases and minerals. You cannot continue to live without water, which makes up about 75% of your body and the world around you. You can acquire water either by the food you consume or just by drinking it. Carbon dioxide, a gas that you produce constantly, is required to be expelled from your body while oxygen is required to be present so that you can produce energy. **Minerals** are necessary for certain reactions in the body and also are critical for transporting substances. Your body needs the mineral iron, for example, because it moves oxygen around your bloodstream.

 BOIL IT DOWN 1.2 If you are interested in discovering more information about the types of interactions of atoms, search chemical bonds.

BIOTIC = LIVING

The **biotic** factors of any ecosystem include all the living organisms—and their behaviors—that affect other living organisms and their environment. To begin our understanding of this, we must first define "living." Life is not defined by one simple or absolute sentence; since life has been evolving for over 3.5 billion years, there are many characteristics and attributes of living things.

You can determine whether something is **living** or not by observing the following attributes: it is made up of cells; it moves; it uses energy; it grows/develops; it responds/adapts to its environment; or it reproduces. A biotic factor is any activity of a living organism that affects another living organism. Biotic factors can negatively affect the populations of organisms but they are also essential to the balance of life within the given ecosystem.

 BOIL IT DOWN 1.3 If you are interested in discovering more in depth information about the elements that you are made of, search elements in living organisms.

A BRIEF LESSON ON LIFE

For the purposes of this course, you need to have a basic understanding of what it means to be living. This is because the human body requires so many living organisms—nutrients—to function.

First, we refer to all living things as **organisms. Cells** are the basic unit of life. All organisms are separated from the outside world by a common barrier called the **cell membrane**. This barrier is selective in what it allows to come and go. Cells must be able to obtain substances such as energy from the outside world. As you will see, the two main types of energy used by organisms are light energy and chemical energy.

All cells are dynamic compartments that constantly need to import materials for their use and also export other substances to maintain their environment. This process is called **homeostasis** (TBCL).

Additionally, cells can't just hang out in their environment. Instead, they must be able to sense information about their surroundings and respond to this information. Two of the most important pieces of information that cells respond to are no surprise:

1) Where the nutrients are located; and
2) Where their mate is located.

 BOIL IT DOWN 1.4 If you are interested in discovering more information about cellular structures, search prokaryotic and eukaryotic cells.

Another important thing you need to know about cells is that they house within them the most important molecule of life called deoxyribose nucleic acid (DNA). **DNA** is the universal inheritance molecule, which dictates the characteristics of an organism. DNA also instructs the organism on how to reproduce. There are two different reproduction strategies on earth:

1) Sexual reproduction is where the DNA of each parent is mixed together to produce an offspring.
2) Asexual reproduction is where the parent makes a copy of itself. This is also known as cloning.

 CHEW ON THIS 1.2 Sex, in common usage, means copulation, whereas in biology it means the exchange of DNA.

Regardless of the size of an organism—whether it's a microscopic single-celled organism or a multicellular organism like us—all life has to mature/develop/grow into what we consider an adult form.

 EXERCISE YOUR BRAIN 1.1 Take a guess how many elements make up your body. Then search online and write down the four most common elements in your body, and give an example of a substance found in your body for each of the elements.

Lastly, all groups of organisms can evolve and have done so from a universal common ancestor. **Evolution** is defined as the change in a population or group over time.

 CHEW ON THIS 1.3 Evolution is not something that occurs within an individual. Individuals do not evolve. Evolution is a group process. If an individual influences this process, it is only in that it has offspring that survive to also reproduce. Evolution, therefore, is a generational influence rather than a moment in time.

 EXERCISE YOUR BRAIN 1.2 Create a list of the characteristics of life; try to use as few words as possible.

A LITTLE BIT ABOUT CELLS AND MICROBES

Your body is not only made up of more than 200 different cell types and trillions of your own cells, but it also has an intimate relationship to **microbes**, which are any organisms we can't see with our eyes. One microbe we will discuss at length during this course is bacteria. **Bacteria** as a group date back 3.5 million years and are the oldest living form of life, pre-dating dinosaurs by hundreds of millions of years.

Microbes inhabit every surface of your body inside and out, are invisible to the eye, and millions can live on the eye of a needle. For every one of your body's own cells, there are 10 microbes living on your body! Most of these microbes are very simplistic cells that resemble the common universal ancestor. These cells are called **prokaryotes**. The name prokaryote originates from the manner in which its DNA is packaged; pro-karyotes' DNA is located within the cell fluid. In more complex organisms, which have only been evolving for half as long as prokaryotes, DNA is compartmentalized into an area called the nucleus. These multicel-lular organisms are called **eukaryotes**. Their cells have many specialized compartments called organelles (little organs!) that establish a division of labor and allow for much more intricate functions enabling these organisms to be much larger than prokaryotes.

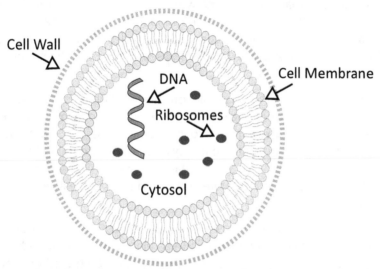

Simple and common structures of prokaryotic cells

For all organisms, whether prokaryotic or eukaryotic, DNA holds the instruction for producing everything that makes us unique but also everything that makes us similar. DNA ultimately does this by instructing the production of substances called proteins. As we delve into what you eat, you will understand how this affects how different cells will turn on or off the production of these proteins. So beware, you are ultimately in charge of your protein destiny.

 CHEW ON THIS 1.4 Prebiotics and probiotics are commercial products that contain either natu-rally occurring or genetically modified microbes to help reinstate or promote healthy microbes in your body.

 EXERCISE YOUR BRAIN 1.3 Draw a picture of the common structures found in prokaryotic cells. Draw a picture of the common structures found in the eukaryotic cells. Describe the general functions of these structures as well as the main difference between prokaryotic and eukaryotic cells.

BASIC INTERACTIONS BETWEEN ORGANISMS

FOOD FOR THOUGHT

There are many biotic interactions we will discuss, but first we are going to touch upon the very intimate relationships of the microbes that live in and on your body to highlight all the potential interactions that exist in your ecosystem.

When two species live in close proximity, these are considered **symbiotic** organisms. The relationship doesn't have to be beneficial to both species; instead symbiosis simply implies that the two species interact for a great deal of their lives or a portion of their life cycle. Not all interactions are considered symbiotic, but all the interactions your body has with microbes are considered symbiotic.

There are four categories of biotic interaction: commensalism, mutualism, exploitation, and competition. There are some interactions where one species profits from the interaction but the other species is not affected (it receives no harm nor any benefit). This is referred to as **commensalism**. If you have ever seen an oyster, you will have noticed that there are many organisms, such as barnacles, living on the oyster shell. The barnacles get a home, the oyster shell—but the barnacle doesn't have any effect on the oyster, good or bad. The interaction of certain species can be advantageous for both; this type of relationship is considered **mutualistic**. We have mutualistic relationships with our pets. We benefit from their companionship and they get a home and get fed.

Another interaction between species—for example, our bodies with microbes—is **exploitation**. This is where one organism profits and the other one is damaged. Examples of exploitative relationships are **herbivorism** (organisms eat vegetation), **predation** (organisms eat animals), and **parasitic** (organisms live on or in another organism and causes harm). All the microbes that fall into this category of exploitation can hurt us and result in disease. As humans, you are already familiar with the concepts of herbivorism and predation because you are likely both an herbivore and a predator if you eat vegetables and meat. We will discuss these in more detail later.

The last category of relationship between species is **competition**, where the interaction of two or more species is unfavorable to all involved. These relationships always involve the reduction of a resource to both species resulting in an expenditure of time and energy to battle the other species. In other words, in competitive relationships, both species would be better off if the other did not exist. Sometimes the result can be devastating for one species, even resulting in their extinction from the area. Competition is a factor in agricultural settings as it comes into play often when trying to grow a crop or raise an animal for meat. For example, say you inherit some land in the country and decide you want to farm it. Corn doesn't grow naturally on the land, but you artificially populate this natural area with this organism (corn) by planting it and feeding it so it will grow. To do this, you will have removed the plants and other organisms that may have grown there naturally. To thrive, they will now have to compete with the corn for resources.

 BOIL IT DOWN 1.5 If you are interested in discovering more information and examples about how of species interact, search commensalism, mutualism, exploitation, and competition.

 EXERCISE YOUR BRAIN 1.4 For all four species interactions, find an example related to microbes and their interaction with your body or to one another that affects you.

TROPHISM: WHO EATS WHOM (AND WHAT DO THEY GET OUT OF IT)

FOOD FOR THOUGHT

As we move onto bigger topics related to food, we will discuss many of the organisms that you are consuming in one form or another. This requires an understanding of how food is created and moved throughout the larger ecosystems of life. More importantly, it is good to know what food is! On a basic level, **food** is an organic molecule that can be utilized for energy production or for general function. In other words, food is used as the ingredients to build necessary substances and perform essential functions within a cell. Food helps your body survive because we need its nutrients to make energy.

Organisms have four different strategies to create or acquire food. When you think of food, you might picture aisles of products that you bring home from the grocery store and eat, or the substances prepared for you and presented on a plate for your enjoyment. It's true that both those images represent food. But it is imperative to recognize that all food, except for synthetic substances, comes from other living organisms. The food that provides your cells with the nutrients it needs (not synthetic/packaged food) is living. The trophic system illustrates this concept that life requires other life.

 EXERCISE YOUR BRAIN 1.5 For all four nutritional strategies, find an organism that fits into each category. Describe the organism's complexity, habitat, and reproductive strategy.

PRODUCERS (AUTOTROPHS) AND CONSUMERS (HETEROTROPHS)

The **trophic system** describes the production of food where producers take in inorganic carbon in the form of carbon dioxide and manufacture food, allowing that food to be available to the consumer. A consumer then eats a producer and utilizes these wonderful substances. Then another consumer will eat that consumer, further moving these substances through each level of the trophic system. For each successive level of the trophic system, including the producers, this organic substance will be recycled, releasing it as carbon dioxide to make it available again to the producers for future manufacturing. All of life—every consumer—relies on the producers to take inorganic carbon in the form of carbon dioxide and make food for the rest of us. We take that food and release it as inorganic carbon. It's a cycle because the producers use it again. Producers take in a form of energy that makes energy available to the rest of us. Mainly we rely on the producers who use light energy. Life requires that the producers within an ecosystem support all other life forms, who are considered consumers (you and me!).

 BOIL IT DOWN 1.6 If you are interested in discovering more in-depth information about the types of nutritional strategies, search for an example of the four nutritional strategies of organisms.

Producers, also called autotrophs, are any organism that can manufacture organic substances that sustain all other life. This means that **autotrophic** organisms take in carbon dioxide and manufacture an **organic** substance, which is defined as any substance that has a carbon atom and a hydrogen atom. Some autotrophs are able to perform these reactions with light energy and are, therefore, called **photoautotrophs**. Other autotrophs utilize chemical energy to create organic molecules and are called **chemoautotrophs**. In either strategy, the resulting organic molecules are necessary for a variety of actions within an organism.

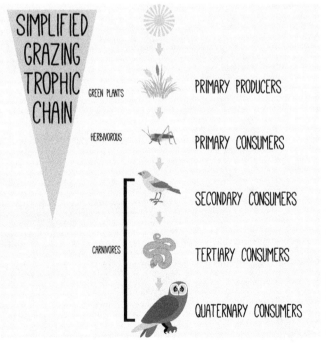

SIMPLIFIED GRAZING TROPHIC CHAIN

GREEN PLANTS — PRIMARY PRODUCERS

HERBIVOROUS — PRIMARY CONSUMERS

SECONDARY CONSUMERS

CARNIVORES — TERTIARY CONSUMERS

QUATERNARY CONSUMERS

© alinabel/Shutterstock.com

CHEW ON THIS 1.5 The word organic has different meanings depending on who is using it. A scientist refers to anything that is organic as being a substance with at least a carbon and hydrogen atom. To be certified organic in the food industry, products must contain only organically-produced ingredients and processing aids, but no other ingredients or additives. It must contain at least 95% organically produced ingredients with the remaining 5% following strict ingredient regulations. The product must be grown, handled, and processed without the use of pesticides or other synthetic chemicals, irradiation, fertilizers made with synthetic ingredients, or bioengineering.

We don't fall into the autotrophic category; we are **heterotrophs**, meaning we have to consume other organisms that contain the organic substances that our cells need—such as sugars, fats, proteins, etc.—already manufactured. We then need to break these organic substances down into small enough pieces to get them into our bodies/cells in order to then reassemble them into larger substances that allow us to function. For example, we eat meat to get proteins, but they are too large to absorb directly from the meat. Therefore, we break down the protein into smaller pieces called amino acids, which we can take into our cells to make our own proteins that make our cells structurally sound. In Section 3, you will learn how you obtain and use these nutrients in your body.

Just like autotrophs, heterotrophs also come in two forms. **Photoheterotrophs** use light energy to break down the larger organic molecules for their own use. We are **chemoheterotrophs**, which means we use chemical energy to break down our food. This is the reason you have your digestive system: to produce the chemicals necessary to break down your food so that you can absorb those substances necessary to sustain life.

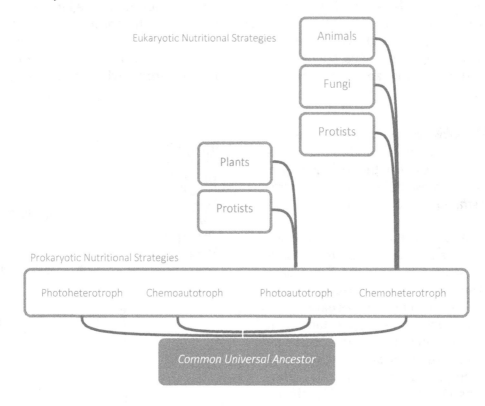

Essentially, in all of the living world, organisms need energy to survive. The means by which an organism gets that energy will put it in either the category of autotroph or heterotroph. Here's a quick and dirty comparison:

	Autotroph	Heterotroph
Produces own food	Yes	No
Types	Photoautotroph, Chemoautotroph	Photoheterotroph, Chemoheterotroph
Examples	Prokaryotes, plants, and algae	Prokaryotes, herbivores, omnivores, and carnivores
Definition	Organisms that can form nutritional organic substances/energy from simple inorganic substances such as carbon dioxide	Organisms that cannot produce organic compounds and must rely on consuming other organisms for nutrition/energy
Where it gets energy/food	Produce their own food for energy	Eat other organisms to get food for energy

 BOIL IT DOWN 1.7 If you are interested in discovering more in depth information about the types of nutritional strategies, search for an example of the four nutritional strategies of organisms.

GETTING ENERGY FROM FOOD

Thus far, we have described, in simple terms, the production or transfer of food in the form of organic molecules. Now, we need to connect this to the next part of trophism in which we follow the process of creating and transferring energy during the interactions of all organisms within an ecosystem.

In attempting to follow the food in an ecosystem, you may have heard it described as a food chain, which is simply a description of who eats whom in a series. In reality, however, most species' interactions are not limited to just one food type. In ecosystems, therefore, it is more relevant to think of a food web, which describes all the producers in an ecosystem and who eats them and one another over the course of all species' interactions. This brings up an important factor that we don't really think about as often as we should: the transfer of energy as a part of our food.

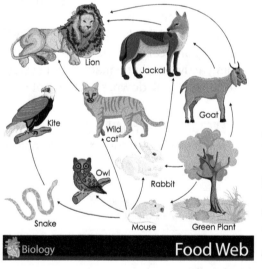
© snapgalleria/Shutterstock

 CHEW ON THIS 1.6 A food web is how we illustrate all of the organisms whose diets impact other organisms. Organisms fall into three basic categories: producers, consumers, or decomposers.

Getting the organic substances that we require is essential, but so is the energy that we derive from our food. When you think of energy in terms of nutrition, you probably associate it with calories, which is appropriate. However, our nutritional needs are not just isolated to the concept of calories. More on calories later. (TBCL)

CHEW ON THIS 1.7 Wrap your head around the word "calorie" versus "Calorie." In science the capital "C" represents a kilocalorie, which is actually the energy level on which your body works. On a food label, a "calorie" is actually kilocalorie. One (1) kilocalorie is the same as one (1) Calorie (upper case C). So one 1 kcal= 1,000 calories. Or when your exercise tracker or fitness machine says you burn about 100 Calories for every mile you jog, it means 100 kilocalories.

ENERGY

Energy is the inherent quality to cause change. All the energy available in the universe has remained the same since the beginning of its existence. Since there is a limit in the amount of energy, the energy out there is not created or destroyed; it merely changes forms. So what forms of energy exist? Energy is either being used and causing change, which is called **kinetic energy**, or it is being stored and waiting to be used, which is called **potential energy**. There are many types of energy that can move between being potential or kinetic, but the three that most relate to your body and nutrition the most are chemical, thermal, and electromagnetic energy (specifically light!).

 CHEW ON THIS 1.8 Two hundred calories in one food is not the same as 200 calories in another food! Think about being faced with the choice of consuming a 100-calorie apple or a 100-calorie soda. From the soda, you get 100 calories plus two nutrients: elevated levels of sodium and sugar. From the apple you get 100 calories plus many nutrients: naturally occurring levels of protein, fat, sodium, carbs, sugars, fiber, vitamins and minerals. When you eat the apple, the good microbes in your body increase, but if you drink the soda the good microbes are diminished.

Just like other organisms, we use both potential and kinetic energy. In the world of physics, we know that the universe is expanding, essentially pulling things apart and fighting against order. However, our cells must have order, so we require a lot of energy—both potential and kinetic—because our cells and bodies are constantly challenged by the natural order of the universe, which is always trying to achieve chaos. One easy way to wrap your head around this concept is to think about a car. If you don't add gas, change the oil, and repair broken parts, eventually that car will not function and slowly it will deteriorate over time. Your body and cells are the same as that car. If you aren't vigilant about doing regular maintenance, performing activities that enhance your systems, and fueling your body with what it needs, then your body's systems will break down, affecting not only your quality of life, but also your longevity.

 EXERCISE YOUR BRAIN 1.6 Knowing what you know about energy, imagine what would happen if the sun disappeared tomorrow. Write down some of the things you envision and some specific impacts.

GET THE SKINNY

Abiotic—any substance that is not organic (e.g., gases, water, minerals).

Autotrophic—an organism that can produce its own organic molecules, also known as food, from an abiotic source.

Bacteria—a prokaryotic lineage of organisms that can interact with your body and used in the production of food (TBCL).

Biotic—anything that's living + organic substances.

Cell—a self-contained functional unit of life.

Cell Membrane—the barrier that protects cells and manages which substances go in or out.

Chemoautotrophic—organisms that make their own food molecules from chemical energy.

Chemoheterotrophic—(humans!) organisms that use chemical energy to break down the food to smaller bits so that we can absorb it and make our own big molecules out of it. The process of being chemoheterotrophic means that we have to consume already existing organic molecules (which we refer to as food) and break them down using chemical energy.

Commensalistic Relationship—an organism that has a relationship with another organism where one gets something helpful and the other is unaffected. Example: a barnacle on an oyster. The oyster isn't helped out, but the barnacle gets a place to stay.

Competitive Relationship—an interaction between two organisms where it's a disadvantage to both organisms; the interaction will impact resources that both require. Whether it's a habitat or food or other resources, the organisms are impacting the availability of those resources. They would both be better off if the other didn't exist.

DNA—the molecule of inheritance.

Ecosystem—any defined area with all its biotic and abiotic components.

Energy—the inherent quality to cause change. Kinetic energy is energy that's being used. Potential energy is energy that's being stored.

Eukaryotes—any organism that has a complex, compartmentalized cellular structure.

Evolution—the process of change in groups at the basic level populations over time.

Exploitive Relationship—one organism profits and the other is harmed to varying degrees. Examples are herbivores, predators, and parasites.

Food—an organic molecule that can be used for energy production.

Food Web—a diagram of the food relationships among species in an ecosystem. It's different from a food chain, which shows only the organisms that are the diet of a top consumer.

Herbivore—an organism that eats vegetation.

Heterotrophic—an organism that must consume other organisms in order to obtain organic molecules.

Homeostasis—the ability to maintain the internal space of a cell the maintenance of substances into the cell. Same is true from a cell to a body.

Microbes—any organism that is too small to see with your eye.

Minerals—an elemental substance found as a salt, ion or within other molecules which is required by your body.

Mutualistic Relationship—a relationship between two organisms that is helpful to both of them in some aspect. Example: There are tons of microbes that live in our gut. They get food because everything we consume isn't digested. They live in our gut and are fed, but they, in turn, produce vitamins for us so we get the benefit of getting vitamins that we couldn't produce on our own.

Organic—any substance that has at least one carbon atom and one hydrogen atom.

Organism—any individual thing considered living.

Parasite—an organism that lives on or in another organism and causes harm.

Photoautotrophic—means you can produce your own organic molecule from light energy e.g., plants make food using sunlight.

Photoheterotrophic—organisms use light energy in order to break down the consumed materials. They are mostly in the microbe world.

Predation—an exploitive relationship when an organism eats other animals.

Prokaryotes—an organism with a basic single-celled structure.

Symbiotic—relationship where two organisms interact for a great deal of their life cycles

Trophism—the food chain. The description of how food and nutrients move through different organisms within an ecosystem—essentially who eats whom. It can be described in terms of food, nutrients and energy and how each one of these, respectively, is moved through the ecosystem.

Section 2
WHO IS THAT IN MY CHEESE PUFFS?

The Organisms That Are Our Food

FOOD FOR THOUGHT

Everything you consume is made up of other organisms. The way your body reacts to and interacts with these organisms has a direct impact on you. Don't you want to know what's happening? Here's some information on some of these organisms that we ingest.

EVOLUTION'S INFLUENCE

All organisms evolved from a common universal ancestor. This process of evolution led to all the groups that currently exist, but more importantly, to all the groups that have existed and are now extinct, which comprise an estimated 99% of life. Scientists have been able to date the earliest known fossils of life to have existed some 3.5 to 3.8 billion years ago (sometime in the Paleoarchean era). All life on earth now, from complex human beings to microscopic bacteria, can be traced back to a common universal ancestor because they all share common characteristics including the molecules which run life, the genetic code.

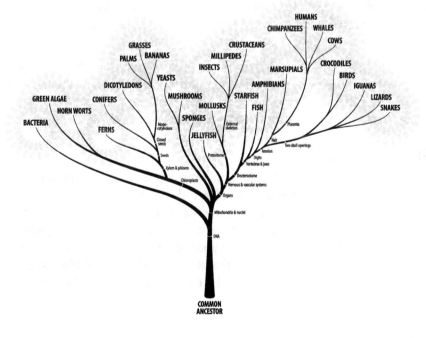

© Zern Liew/Shutterstock

13

Evolution occurs at different levels, but all evolution within a population results in a change in that group of organisms over time. Scientists Charles Darwin and Alfred Russel Wallace famously described the most well-known mechanism for evolution, which is called natural selection. **Natural selection** is the differential survival and reproductive success of some individuals in a population with distinct characteristics due to the influence of their environment. Natural selection needs material to work with, so the populations' genetic variation is an important factor.

Most genetic variation is a result of random mutations (permanent changes in the chemical structure of genes) within DNA, resulting in the introduction of new characteristics. In the end, a population becomes unique from its original population, producing a new group of organisms. Since this process has been going on for billions of years and the earth's environment has changed dramatically, it is easy to see how all these diverse groups of organisms exist. One major distinction between the kinds of life on earth is the prokaryotic versus eukaryotic organisms. Prokaryotes are much more simplistic cells, but they play a major role in food production and food-borne illnesses. Eukaryotes are the organisms you are more familiar with eating as food, so we will explore these in greater detail. Ok, my fellow chemoheterotroph, let's begin to relate this to your needs…

PROKARYOTES WE EAT

The organisms on earth that are called **prokaryotes**—all single-celled organisms—most resemble the universal common ancestor. This group includes bacteria and archaea. Archaea live in extreme environments, and we really don't encounter them very often. Bacteria live all around, on and in us. There are bacteria unique to different surfaces of our skin, including your belly button.

 BOIL IT DOWN 2.1 If you are interested in all the bacteria on your body, search for the belly button project.

Prokaryotes are critical to our existence. If humans disappeared from earth tomorrow, life would go on for most other species. If, however, prokaryotes disappeared tomorrow, the future survival of all other life forms would be in peril. This is because prokaryotes are critical in obtaining and recycling of chemical elements in ecosystems.

Chemoheterotrophic prokaryotes are decomposers, who break down corpses, dead vegetation, and waste products and unlock supplies of carbon, nitrogen, and other elements that are essential for life. They are also instrumental in turning elements from non-living environmental factors into essential organic compounds. For example, nitrogen-fixing bacteria are able to harness atmospheric nitrogen, which no other organism is able to use naturally.

Autotrophic prokaryotes use carbon dioxide to make organic compounds, which are then passed up through food chains. For example, cyanobacteria are photosynthetic bacteria that are erroneously referred to as blue-green algae, but they are not eukaryotic. They are the oldest known group of organisms that still exist today. Cyanobacteria fossil records date back 3.5 billion years.

PATHOGENIC BACTERIA

Pathogenic substances can cause disease or infection. Most bacteria are not pathogenic, but we hear a lot about pathogenic bacteria and, if you've ever been affected by a pathogenic bacteria—such as *E.coli* or salmonella—you will not soon forget the unpleasantness caused by it. You're probably inclined to focus on the bacteria that does harm to your body such as when you get food poisoning. **Pathogenic bacteria** are found on fresh foods or undercooked foods and can disrupt your normal bodily functions. There are two categories of pathogenic bacteria. **Exotoxins** produce a toxin that is released to the outside and evolved as a defensive substance. **Endotoxins** have harmful substances that are a structural part of the cell.

EXERCISE YOUR BRAIN 2.1 Find examples of the most common food-borne illnesses. Which ones are caused by pathogenic bacteria and what foods are they commonly found on?

Because of harmful bacteria, humans have devised different methods of preservation and cooking to eliminate the risk. Strategies that prevent fresh foods from spoiling include traditional methods such as using salt, pickling using acids, and drying food, as well as the current trend of adding synthetic compounds to increase the shelf life of a product. Cooking also kills off cells. By raising the temperature of fresh foods, the potential pathogens are killed because their cells can't withstand the high temperatures. This process also starts to predigest food for us by breaking apart cells and substances.

 BOIL IT DOWN 2.2 If you are interested in synthetic preservatives, search for common food preservatives online.

GOOD BACTERIA

Be sure not to always focus on the bad bacteria; the good bacteria are just as important if not more important than the bad ones. We can thank bacteria when we enjoy a great cheese plate or yogurt smoothie: bacteria are used to transform milk into yogurt and cheese. Normally, specific bacteria are used to impart different flavors to a cheese such as various species of the genus *Lactococci, Streptococci*, and *Lactobaccilli*. Bacteria are also used to pickle foods. While you may see vinegar on the ingredient list on a jar of pickles, traditionally really well-made pickled products are created using different species of *Lactobaccilli* and the result is delicious.

Also, the mutualistic and commensalistic bacteria in your foods help to increase the levels of microbes that are helpful. During normal consumption of food your microbiome will change and potentially become susceptible to pathogenic bacteria. But the process of repopulation of the microbiome is especially important after taking antibiotics especially wide-spectrum antibiotics, which don't target a pathogenic bacteria but instead kill all the vulnerable bacteria including the good/neutral bacteria. By consuming a good mixture of bacteria such as those found in yogurts with multiple live cultures, your microbiome will become balanced again.

EUKARYOTES WE EAT: PROTISTS, PLANTS, FUNGI, AND ANIMALS

The next large group of organisms are the **eukaryotes**. This is by no means an exhaustive list of every eukaryote, but a sampling to give you a sense of the diversity of this large group, where they live and their roles in your diet. Eukaryotes were once thought to include a single-celled group called **Protista**, as well as plants, fungi and animals. Unfortunately the protists were all lumped together because they were all small. We now know, however, that some protists are plant-like, some are fungal-like, and some are even animal-like. If you were to examine the basic tree of the eukaryotes, there is still a group called the protists, but each lineage of the plant, fungi, and animals also have a single-celled lineage. How do protists really relate to your food? Most of them are not food for you directly, but more often they are the food for your food. For example, fish feed on phytoplankton and protists that live in the water. Since this course focuses on food for your body, this brings us to the three main lineages of food in the eukaryotic lineage: **plants, fungi, and animals**.

 BOIL IT DOWN 2.3 If you are interested in the various evolutionary trees that depict where protists are located on the tree of life, search protist evolutionary tree.

PLANTS: FRUIT, FLOWERS AND VEGETATION

Plants are the base producers for us regardless of whether you are an omnivore, vegetarian, pescatarian, or vegan (see **CHEW ON THIS 2.2**). Plants are broken up into spore-producing plants like mosses and ferns, **gymnosperms** which are cone-bearing plants, and **angiosperms** which are flowering plants. We generally do not eat spore-producing plants; however, some people do eat fiddle-head ferns, which are simply the new fern sprouting up when they are tender. Cone-bearing plants produce some food products such as pine nuts. But the majority of what we eat falls into the category of flowering plants.

 CHEW ON THIS 2.1 Some plants aren't green and aren't producers; instead they are parasitic!

 CHEW ON THIS 2.2 Humans generally choose to follow a particular diet. Omnivores eat meat and vegetables. Vegetarians eat vegetables and dairy. Pescatarians eat fish and vegetables, but won't eat land animals. Vegans eat only vegetables, and will not eat any food that contains anything made from animal, such as eggs or dairy.

Flowering Plant (Angiosperm) Anatomy

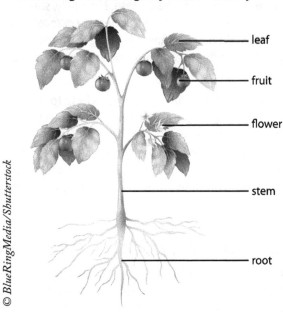

— leaf
— fruit
— flower
— stem
— root

© BlueRingMedia/Shutterstock

 BOIL IT DOWN 2.4 If you are interested in unique plants that don't undergo photosynthesis, search plants that aren't producers.

All green plants are **photoautotrophs**. They need access to light and carbon dioxide and they, like us, require essential nutrients. An **essential nutrient** is any substance that is required by an organism to function but that it can't manufacture itself. The structure of green flowering plants includes roots, stems, leaves, and flowers. **Roots** are the below-ground structures whose purpose is to collect water and the plant's essential nutrients, which include minerals such as phosphorus, nitrogen, and sulfur. These compounds are found in fertilizers, which contain ingredients that help the organism grow, but that aren't readily available. Then there is the **stem**, which is a stalk that protrudes from the ground. The stem provides the plant with the ability to have access to sunlight. Some stems contain cells that can undergo the process of photosynthesis, which is the process of turning light energy into chemical energy resulting in the production of food. It is easy to tell if a plant can or cannot perform photosynthesis by checking whether or not the stem is green. If it is green that means it will be able to manufacture food via photosynthesis.

The other two major structures are located off the stem of the plant: the leaves and the flowers. The **leaves** are the main photosynthetic structures and contain the pores where carbon dioxide can enter to be made into an organic molecule.

The **flowers** are where the magic happens. Most flowering plants are hermaphrodites, meaning they have the ability to produce both sperm and egg. This is extremely advantageous because the plant doesn't need to find a mate to have baby plants. But it is in the plant's best interest to mate with another plant to increase the genetic diversity in the population. Plants, therefore, have evolved some clever methods to attract pollinators. For example, growing colored flower petals; formatting specialized structures that resemble other animals (such as bees); and producing nectar are all strategies that have evolved to attract pollinators. The parent plant also doesn't want to be competing with its own offspring, therefore, they've evolved different seed dispersal strategies including fruit production!

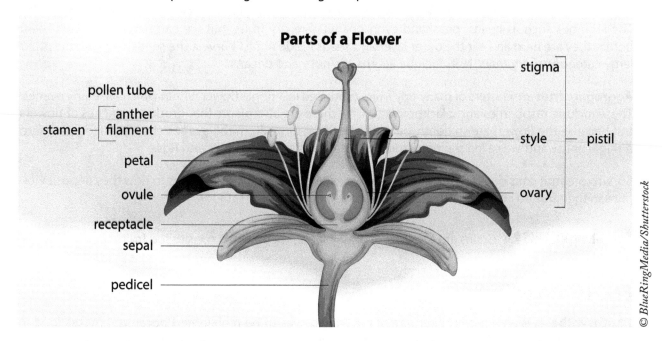

Parts of a Flower

stigma

pollen tube

anther

stamen — filament

petal

ovule

receptacle

sepal

pedicel

style — pistil

ovary

© BlueRingMedia/Shutterstock

Within a **hermaphroditic flower**, there are both male parts and female parts. The male reproductive structure, called the **stamen**, is where sperm are produced. The female reproductive structure is called the **carpel**, which includes the ovary, where the individual egg or multiple eggs reside. Once the egg or eggs are fertilized, they become a seed. Around that seed, the ovary will ripen, and this is what you eat. So, the next time you are looking at the fruit bowl, you might ask yourself, "What ripened ovary am I in the mood for today?" Besides fruit, what other parts of a plant do you eat? We also eat the flower, the vegetation of the plant or a combination of the fruit, the flower and vegetation.

 CHEW ON THIS 2.3 Most vitamins are produced by plant cells and are stored in a special area called a vacuole.

VEGETATION WE EAT

We eat certain above ground vegetation, including leafy greens, celery or the green part of onion-family plants. We also eat below-ground vegetation, which includes three main categories: tubers, roots, and bulbs. **Tubers** are enlargements of the root that will result in a new plant, such as potatoes. **Roots** are simply the below ground portion of the plant such as carrots, beets, or rutabagas. **Bulbs** form in plants that have above ground vegetation that dies, usually because of temperature and light changes. The bulb, for example an onion, is where the plant will store energy in the form of a complex substance called starch. (TBCL)

FLOWERS AND FRUIT WE EAT

The flower is made up of the petals, the reproductive structures (stamen and carpel), and sometimes little leaves at the base. Not all flowers are edible and some may contain compounds that cause digestive issues or even death. From the flower, we get the fruit. There are different types of fruits based upon what contributes to the actual flesh of the fruit. Apples and pears, for instance, are accessory fruit. **Accessory fruits** get their name because the carpel(s) become encapsulated by the stem and form the fruit.

Some fruits are made from one flower with one ovary that grows into the flesh and are aptly named simple fruit. Most fleshy fruit you eat fall into this category including the stone fruit (apricot, peach, nectarine), citrus fruit (lemon, lime, grapefruit), and berries (tomato and grape).

There are fruits where their outer layer becomes hardened to varying degrees; they are called dry fruits. The legumes such as beans, peas, and even peanuts are dry fruits, but we can harvest some of them before they are hard and eat the outer layer and seeds inside or just harvest the seeds. Nuts are the other large category of dry fruits. Nuts include acorns, walnuts, and pecans.

Aggregate fruit are clusters of many tiny fruits produced in a single flower within which are many ovaries. These include raspberries and blackberries. Lastly, there are also plants that produce bunches of flowers but because the flowers are so tightly packed when fruit forms from the ovaries, they fused together into a single entity and are called multiple fruit. Two examples are pineapples and figs.

So, why are fruit considered so nutritious? We will explore this later, but it relates to how they deposit vitamins in their fruit to continue attracting seed-dispersing animals! (TBCL)

 CHEW ON THIS 2.4 Grains are seeds from grass plants. They are still considered fruit seeds.

PHOTOSYNTHESIS

Photosynthesis is an amazing phenomenon that deserves to be highlighted because it makes food in the form of plants so valuable to us and other consumers. The origin of all organic material comes from our wonderful producers at the bottom/base of all our food webs. These organisms are mostly photoautotrophs, which as you know means that they use light as their main source of energy for food production and can use carbon dioxide as their main source of carbon. So, all the green plants that you observe throughout your day are supporting you by taking in carbon dioxide and, eventually, through either themselves directly or via other consumers, will provide you with the food you need. This is why some people are compelled to hug trees—just being grateful! The process these organisms use to produce organic matter is called photosynthesis.

The best way to understand photosynthesis is by separating the steps into the "photo" stage and the "synthesis" stage. To understand how these stages work, you must have a general grasp of what a reaction is. A **reaction** is any process by which a **reactant**(s) or starting substance(s) is/are transformed into product(s) or the end substance(s). Each stage of photosynthesis is necessary but each has a very different and distinct outcome, both of which are necessary for the production of organic molecules. Both stages are aptly named. The "photo" stage refers to light and hence occurs when light energy is transformed first into electricity and then into chemical energy. The "synthesis" stage refers to a combination and occurs when carbon dioxide is assembled into an organic molecule.

 BOIL IT DOWN 2.5 If you are interested in learning more about the intricate structure of chloroplasts and the photosystems, search light and dark reactions of photosynthesis.

PROCESS OF PHOTOSYNTHESIS

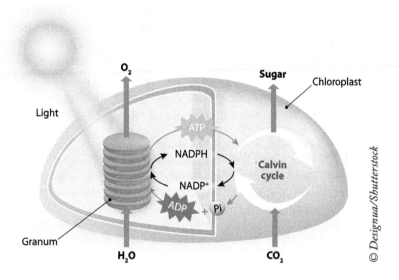

© Designua/Shutterstock

 CHEW ON THIS 2.5 The photo stage is often referred to as the light reactions, whereas the synthesis stage is called the dark reactions or the Calvin cycle.

THE PHOTO STAGE

Although much can be said about the process, let's go ahead and ruin the ending of the photo stage: this stage results in three very cool substances being produced: adenosine triphosphate (**ATP**), nicotinamide adenine dinucleotide phosphate (**NADPH**), and oxygen gas! Yes, this is where all the oxygen that you inhale to survive is created! Ready to hug a tree yet? Oddly, this is a **by-product**, meaning that it isn't necessary for the reactions of photosynthesis to produce the organic substance.

Chemical Energy Carrier

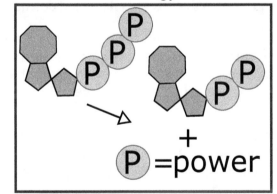

Adenosine Triphosphate

Electrical Energy Carrier

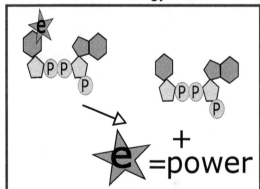

Nicotinamide Adenine
Dinucleotide Phosphate

The other two substances, ATP and NADPH, are substances called energy carriers and both are made of nucleotides, which are the same type of monomer (subunit) that makes up your DNA and RNA. Although they function on a microscopic level, what they do is an actual physical process similar to what a storage and delivery company does. These companies come and gather your items, either deliver them immediately, or store them until you request delivery. ATP and NADPH are doing the same thing. ATP is important because it's the universal (meaning for all organisms!) energy carrier that powers the reactions of your cells. ATP carries and delivers a soon-to-be famous material called a **phosphate group** (TBCL). Most reactions in all organisms receive the phosphate group, which energizes the reaction, allowing it to proceed. NADPH is a different type of energy carrier. It facilitates a limited amount of reactions by donating electrons, which energizes the reaction.

Let's look at where these processes take place in order to understand how they take place. We know that green plants carry out photosynthesis, and that the green pigment is important to their ability to do this. The green cells have a specialized organelle called a **chloroplast**. Within the chloroplast there are membranes in which pigments are embedded.

 BOIL IT DOWN 2.6 If you are more interested in pigments, search naturally occurring pigments or synthetically produced pigments.

 CHEW ON THIS 2.6 Each green plant cell will have many chloroplasts, and a plant can increase or decrease the amount based upon demand.

The **pigments** are a part of the working mechanism called a **photosystem**. These pigments are arranged in a specific pattern to help the organelle efficiently harness light energy and produce chemical energy. The pigments will collect light energy from the sun and generate electricity. This electricity will move on to the other part of the photosystem, called an **electron transport chain**. Sound fancy? Well, just think of the electron transport chain as an electrical wire. The end result of plugging in a lamp will result in light being produced by the electricity in the cord. The end result of the electron transport chain will be the production of chemical energy in the form of ATP and NADPH!

 EXERCISE YOUR BRAIN 2.2 Think of objects around you and list ones that have pigments and describe what you think they do with the energy.

What about the oxygen? Well the photosystem relies on a constant supply of electrons for its electricity. The pigment responsible for gathering these electrons is called chlorophyll a. It is responsible for the actual conversion of light into electricity by ripping electrons from water (H2O). When it does this, it will generate oxygen gas as a byproduct.

Photo stage overview: Photosystems are made up of pigments and an electron transport chain. Pigments will collect light energy. **Chlorophyll a** will remove electrons from water creating oxygen gas as a byproduct and supplying the electron transport chain with an energized electron creating the energy carriers ATP and NADPH. Boom!

 CHEW ON THIS 2.7 A pigment is any substance that can absorb light energy and convert it to either heat energy, light energy, chemical energy or even fluorescence.

THE SYNTHESIS STAGE

Now that we have ATP and NADPH, they will move onto the synthesis stage of this critical process. The "synthesis" reactions occur in the fluid of the chloroplast. This is a cyclical series of reactions that starts with a crucial step called **carbon fixation**. This involves carbon dioxide being incorporated into an organic molecule. Next, the resulting organic molecule is stabilized and energized by NADPH dropping off its electron and ATP donating its phosphate group. This will result in an organic substance with one new carbon atom extracted from the carbon dioxide. Then ATP will recycle the original organic molecule to start the cycle again. The end result of this cycle is the production of a sugar. This sugar is the basic building block in plants because it can be used to produce energy (ATP) or to build other molecules for the plant that are structural (such as phospholipids of the membrane) or functional (such as proteins, which transport substances around the plant). They all can be manufactured using the food produced by the "synthesis" stage.

 CHEW ON THIS 2.8 For the "synthesis" stage to produce a glucose molecule, a 6 carbon molecule, the plant must perform the cycle six times.

Synthesis stage overview: Carbon dioxide is acquired through pores in the plant. It will be used in a series of reactions starting with carbon fixation to produce an energized sugar thanks to the help of ATP and NADPH produced in the "photo" reactions. In the end, organic material in now available to the consumers we will discuss next!

 BOIL IT DOWN 2.7 If you are interested in learning more about different type of plants, search C3, C4 and CAM plants.

 EXERCISE YOUR BRAIN 2.3 Make a concept map of the different components of photosynthesis.

FUNGI

On to the fungi! If you thought mushrooms were the only fungi you can eat, you would be wrong. **Fungi** are found as single-celled organisms called **yeast** that are really important in your food and food production. An obvious example of yeast you eat is bread. The process by which bread rises is fascinating and it's yeast that makes it happen! These organisms have the option of either producing energy with or without oxygen. When they do it without oxygen, the process is called **fermentation** and specifically, in bread, they undergo alcohol fermentation. So, as the dough is warmed, these little guys start to produce carbon dioxide and alcohol, allowing the bread to get air bubbles inside. The alcohol during the process of baking the bread is baked off, however, when we make wine or beer, we use this same process! Depending on the type of yeast and the food you provide it, you will get a combination of alcohol and flavor in a beverage. Fungi also are used in cheese making and many other prominent food products.

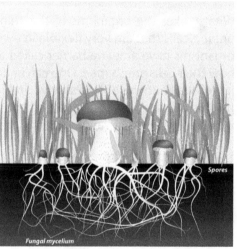

© Designua/Shutterstock

BOIL IT DOWN 2.8 If you are interested in the role of fungi as nutrient recyclers, search mycorrhizal fungi.

In a big picture view, fungi are extremely important recyclers called decomposers. Most fungi live underground as very small threads. These threads are the true **decomposers**, which are organisms that degrade any dead or dying organisms to recycle their nutrients for the rest of us to use. You only see fungi when they are going to reproduce sexually, which is when mushrooms grow above ground. Mushrooms are the vehicle that the underground fungi use to disperse spores that result in new organisms. There are two types of mushrooms: those that are edible and those that can make you very sick or even kill you.

To prevent predation, different mushrooms and plants evolved methods to dissuade you from eating them. Toxin-production would prevent predation and, therefore, natural selection would prefer you to survive! But not all substances in mushrooms will kill you; some, similar to the compounds produced by onions or peppers, merely cause brief discomfort.

 CHEW ON THIS 2.9 The same individual fungus organism (genetically tested, of course) can penetrate the ground across many hundreds of miles. Pretty cool!

Okay, so at this point if you are a vegan or vegetarian, the consumption of the following will not apply. But you should know about it anyway, so read on…

ANIMALS WE EAT: INVERTEBRATES AND VERTEBRATES

Animals come in two main groups: those without a backbone (**invertebrates**) and those with a backbone (**vertebrates**). Humans eat them all. In some cases we may eat the entire organism, while in other cases only a portion of the organism such as the **meat** (meaning the muscles), or even, oddly, the gonads.

What makes the organisms of the animal kingdom so different from other organisms? Well, we have unique cells that are very flexible in comparison to the other groups we have discussed. All those other organisms have an extra barrier called a cell wall. This affords them a lot of protection, but it also limits how their cells are shaped. One can imagine that an ancient eukaryotic cell, through some mutation, lost its cell wall but was able to survive and reproduce. This led to the many different lineages of animals. Our flexible cells are able to latch together into tissues that then combine into our multiple organs resulting in unique organisms of various forms. But let's get back to munching on animals.

INVERTEBRATES WE EAT

Within the invertebrates, the major subcategories that humans consume are the bivalves, cephalopods, gastropods, crustaceans, insects, and even echinoderms. There are cultures that even consume spiders and worms, round, flat and segmented! Please note, this section focuses on examples of the invertebrates that we eat; it is not a lesson on invertebrates.

Molluscs

Let's start with those that are most related to one another. Bivalves, cephalopods and gastropods are within the same group called **molluscs**. One striking feature common to almost all molluscs is the production of a hardened substance. In bivalves, this is very apparent in the form of two shells connected by a hinge. This group has the important food organisms: oysters, mussels, clams, and scallops. Molluscs are also most likely to be found in the water. The cephalopods include the octopus and squid, which are eaten by many different cultures. This group has many unique characteristics including a very complex nervous system and eyes. Cephalopods produce a hardened beak that helps them feed. Gastropods, such as snails, conches, and slugs have a shell and a soft body. With a few exceptions in the water-living and shell-producing molluscs, as well as some snails and slugs in the gastropod group, we usually don't eat the entire organism. The land snail includes the delicious French dish escargot. For most bivalves and gastropods, humans eat the entire organism excluding, of course, the shells in which they abide. In the cephalopods, humans usually consume the tentacles, which are the appendages of the animal. For some squid and baby octopi, however, we consume the entire body.

Arthropods: Crustaceans and Insects

Other invertebrate organisms we consume fall into the class of **arthropods**, which includes crustaceans and insects. All arthropods have a unique set of characteristics, most prominently a skeleton called an exoskeleton that is on the outside (instead of on the inside). It is made up of a hard polysaccharide (TBLC) called chitin that is layered to form a hard protective barrier. All of these organisms have paired appendages, which they mainly use for movement, but some are specialized for feeding, protection, and even reproduction.

Crustaceans are the familiar crab, lobster, shrimp, and crayfish. In lobster and crayfish, the main meat, which is the muscle tissue of the animal, we eat is the tail and appendage meat although some people will suck the juice out of the head of the crayfish! Crab can either be consumed by retrieving the muscles within the body cavity or, when they are molting, the crab's soft and can be prepared through removing the innards (mainly the gills and the reproductive-portion of the shell). Shrimp can often be eaten whole including the shell, or they are prepared by removing the tail and the shell and deveining them.

Insects are not commonly consumed in the United States, but there are some cultures that, because the swarms or populations of insects are so large and invasive, the people are inclined to eat them. The most commonly consumed insects are grasshoppers, crickets, stink bugs, beetles, butterflies, moths and ants. This practice is not only practical but also very nutritious. These animals are usually high in protein, fiber, minerals, and vitamins while at the same time being low calorie snacks.

This covers the main invertebrates that you might consume, so let's take a look at the vertebrates that might find their way into your diet.

VERTEBRATES WE EAT: MEAT AND FISH

Vertebrates are different from other animals because they have a backbone, which signifies a complex nervous system. Along with intricate sensory systems, other complex features have evolved in the vertebrates such as their digestive, reproductive, urinary, circulatory, and immune systems, each of which has unique characteristics. They also have an internal skeleton called an endoskeleton, which is made up of bone or cartilage. What vertebrates do we eat? Meat and fish comprise this category, so let's take a closer look.

Meat

The major types of meat (again meaning the muscle tissue of an animal) we consume are poultry, including chickens (either laying hens or broilers), turkeys and ducks; cow, including the cattle for meat, young calves used to produce veal, and dairy cattle; swine (pig); and sheep, including juveniles called lambs. On average, an American consumes 180 pounds of meat per year—mainly beef, veal, pork, chicken, turkey, and lamb—whereas an American only consumes 15 pounds of seafood, including our water-loving vertebrates, the fish.

 BOIL IT DOWN 2.9 If you are interested in free-range cattle production, search open-range cattle farming.

Most land animals consumed for meat in the United States are now raised in factory farms called **CAFO**s (concentrated animal feeding operations). These animals usually are confined to a small area where they defecate, eat and even live among dead animals instead of being allowed to graze and move about their environment. These animals are not fed what they would normally consume if they were free, but instead they eat a specialized patented mixture.

 CHEW ON THIS 2.10 Certified organic farms do not allow CAFOs. Depending on the type of animal, they must have access to a certain amount of space as well as access to vegetation that they would eat if they were in their natural environment.

Fish

The other group of vertebrates that we consume are fresh- and salt-water (marine) fish. Like their land-loving brethren, fish are consumed mainly for the meat. Fish range in size in terms of both length and weight. Some, like the sardine or anchovy are eaten whole—guts, bones and all because they are so small! And others are eaten as a delicacy including the gonads such as the shad roe and eggs referred to as caviar, which typically come from threatened fish species such as the sturgeon.

Many of the fish we eat for meat transition in size throughout their life cycles and can have a very valuable impact on the organisms in their aquatic food webs. For instance, many fish begin life as primary consumers in the food web and as they grow through juvenile stages into full adults they can either remain a primary consumer or get so large that they become a secondary or even, as in the case with sharks, a quaternary consumer. At all levels, the balance of a local food web relies on the populations of the lower levels of the trophic system, which is why overfishing can become a huge impact on the survival of other organisms within that food web. For instance, fishing practices can affect the bivalve and crab population that can affect the turtle populations and the osprey, bald eagle, and the heron populations. Hence you can see the interrelatedness of both animals you eat to animals you may admire.

 EXERCISE YOUR BRAIN 2.4 Make a table of the major groups of organisms you consume; in the first column list the groups, in the next column indicate whether they are consumers or producers, in the next column indicate what type of habitat they can be found, and in the last column indicate if we cultivate those organisms.

 EXERCISE YOUR BRAIN 2.5 Examine the food you eat throughout one day. List all the different organisms that contribute to these foods. Break them up into bacteria, protists (not likely so don't worry if you can't find these), plants, fungi, and animals.

GET THE SKINNY

Accessory Fruit—fruit whose carpels are encapsulated by the fruit flesh, e.g., apples.

Aggregate Fruit—clusters of many fruit from a single ovary, e.g., raspberries and figs.

Arthropods—invertebrates, including crustaceans and insects.

ATP—adenosine triphosphate is the universal energy carrier molecule.

CAFOs (concentrated animal feeding operations)—factory farms that raise animals in an environment vastly different from what they naturally require to thrive.

Carbon Fixation—the reaction of incorporating a carbon atom from an inorganic substance (carbon dioxide) and making it organic.

Chlorophyll—a special pigment that gives plants their green appearance.

Decomposers—organisms that degrade any dead or dying organisms to recycle their nutrients for the rest of us to use.

Dry Fruit—fruit with hardened outer layer, e.g., legumes and nuts.

Electron Transport Chain—a series of reactions that harness energy from electrons.

Endoskeleton—skeleton on the inside.

Endotoxins—pathogenic bacteria contained within the bacteria cell.

Evolution—a change in a group of organisms over time.

Exoskeleton—skeleton on the outside.

Exotoxins—pathogenic bacteria that releases the toxin outside their structure.

Fermentation—process of yeast producing energy without oxygen.

Fungi—an organism that feeds on decomposing organisms.

Gymnosperm—cone-bearing plant.

Hermaphrodite—any individual organism that has both male and female reproductive structures and therefore can produce both sperm and egg.

Invertebrates—animals without a backbone.

Meat—the muscle of an organism.

Molluscs—invertebrates, usually with a hardened covering, i.e. bivalves, cephalopods, gastropods.

NADPH—nicotinamide adenine dinucleotide phosphate is an energy carrier molecule that stores and delivers electrons.

Natural Selection—differential survival and reproductive success of some individuals.

Pathogenic Bacteria—bacteria that can harm you.

Phosphate Group—an important hydrophilic structural component of substances such as DNA and RNA, as well as energy-rich molecules, such as ATP and phospholipids.

Phospholipid—major component of all cell membranes that form a double-layered fatty substance that protects your cells.

Photosynthesis—process of turning light energy into chemical energy to make food.

Photosystem—the functional unit of photosynthesis that converts light energy into chemical energy. Made up of pigments including chlorophyll a and an electron transport chain.

Pigment—any substance which can absorb light energy.

Plants—a group of producers that provide organic matter for most terrestrial consumers.

Protists—single-celled eukaryotes that are free-living and not fungi, plant, or animal (algae).

Reactant—a starting/original substance in a reaction.

Reaction—a process of transforming one substance into a new substance.

Simple Fruit—one flower and one ovary grows into flesh, i.e., stone, citrus and berries.

Vegetation—plants, such as tubers, roots and bulbs.

Vertebrates—animals with a backbone.

Yeast—a fungi capable of converting sugar into alcohol and carbon dioxide.

Section 3
WHERE ARE THOSE TRANS FATS?

What We Get from Other Organisms

FOOD FOR THOUGHT

Now that you know what organisms mainly comprise your diet, you need to really dig deeper into the process of consumption and understand what you are getting from them. Nutrients come in two categories: those that are non-essential and those that are essential. **Non-essential** nutrients are manufactured by your cells using common ingredients that are readily available in your body. In other words, you don't need to get them anywhere else because your body makes enough to function efficiently. **Essential nutrients** are those that you need to function, but that your body can't manufacture, therefore you must obtain them in your food.

Because a goal of this course is to enable you to read and understand a nutrition food label on the food products that you buy, we will explore the main types of nutrients that the government requires be listed on food labels. Food labels are found on the packaging of food and list the nutritional facts of the food. These are mandatory and it's imperative that you understand them if you want to be informed about the ingredients in foods and where they fit into your daily diet. Your good eating habits require that you know how to shop for a healthy diet and compare and contrast different product options.

We will focus on the major nutrients:

- Fats
- Cholesterol
- Carbohydrates
- Sodium
- Protein
- Minerals
- Vitamins

These are the nutrients that your body requires to function and to produce energy. We will describe the general features of these substances, the food they are found in, and their basic uses in your body.

Nutrition Facts

Serving Size
Serving per Container

Amount per Serving		
Calories	Calories from Fat	
% Daily Value*		
Total Fat	g	%
Saturated Fat	g	%
Trans Fat	g	
Cholesterol	g	%
Sodium	g	%
Total Carbohydrate	g	%
Dietary Fiber	g	%
Sugars	g	
Protein	g	
Vitamin A	%	
Vitamin C	%	
Calcium	%	
Iron	%	

*Percent Daily Values are based on a _____ calorie diet.

	Calories		
Total Fat	Less than	g	g
Sat Fat	Less than	g	g
Cholesterol	Less than	mg	mg
Sodium	Less than	mg	mg
Total Carbohydrate		g	g
Dietary Fiber		g	g

 EXERCISE YOUR BRAIN 3.1 Look up the requirements for a nutrition facts label and understand the components and their meanings. And always refer to the food label before making choices—you will be better at it after the course!

FATS

Let's start at the top of the nutrition facts label with the fats. Fats get a bad rap, but the fact is you couldn't live without fat and fatty substances. Every single organism on earth needs fat, because *the cell membrane of every single cell in your body (and every other body) is made of fat*! Fats support your body's most important functions, such as vitamin absorption (TBCL). They are made up of long chains of carbon atoms surrounded by hydrogen (aka hydrocarbons). Think of them as a straw. This particular combination of atoms doesn't like water and is considered **hydrophobic**, which means it will repel water. Fats fall into a larger category of hydrophobic substances called lipids, which all share this characteristic of pushing away water. Because fats repel water, it makes them very hard to transport around our bodies because our main transport tissue, blood, is mainly made up of water.

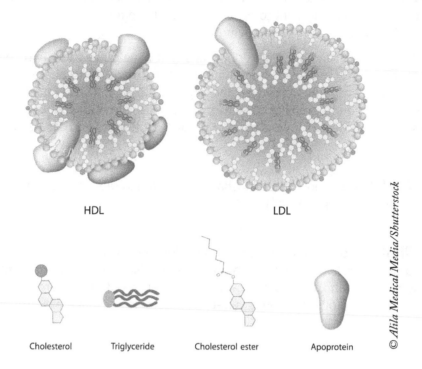

HDL   LDL

Cholesterol   Triglyceride   Cholesterol ester   Apoprotein

© Alila Medical Media/Shutterstock

On the food label, you will notice that there are four potential fats that may be in a food product: saturated fats, monounsaturated fats, polyunsaturated fats, and trans fats.

SATURATED FATS

Let's start with the **saturated fats**, which generally come from terrestrial animals. Going back to the straw analogy, saturated fats are straight straws, and if you have a bunch of them, you can stack them on top of one another. These are not dynamic and are considered lazy because they tend to hang out in a pile of straws. You would be most familiar with them as the white fat you see in meat, and too much of it can raise your blood cholesterol, the substances known as HDL and LDL (TBCL).

CHEW ON THIS 3.1 Unsaturated fats are found in fruits, vegetables, fish, and grains. Saturated fats are found in animal meats along with a few types of tropical fruits. Trans fats are in any product that has hydrogenated oils listed on the ingredients of the nutrition facts label.

UNSATURATED FATS

Monounsaturated and polyunsaturated fats are often referred to as the "good fats" and generally come from plant sources. **Unsaturated fats** are like bendable straws instead of straight straws. The way the carbon chain is combined causes the once-linear-structure to be bent. If the chain is bent once, it is called monounsaturated. If it is bent at two or more locations, then it is considered polyunsaturated, which is a more dynamic substance because the "straws" can't lie flat on one another, therefore, they bounce around one another in a fluid you typically call an oil.

TRANS FATS

So where do trans fats come into play? **Trans fats** are usually artificially created by humans to produce a food product that is solid or semi-solid at room temperature, improving its texture and shelf life and lowering its cost. When trans fats are created, an unsaturated fat undergoes the process of **hydrogenation** (treated with hydrogen). An unsaturated fat can either be fully or partially hydrogenated, transforming the structure of the straw from being bent to becoming straight to resemble saturated fats. As a result, the trans fats are now less dynamic and slow moving.

Trans fats are the "bad fats" and are really "good fats that have gone bad." Two common examples of trans fat products are peanut butter and margarine, which are made from vegetable sources. This process will impart the chemical properties to convert the oily fats into almost solid fats so it can be used in food products? Your body can bring in any of these forms and utilize them for your cells and body to function. Too much trans fat is considered far worse for your blood cholesterol and can result in increased cardio-vascular disease.

 BOIL IT DOWN 3.1 If you are interested in what types of vegetables are used to manufacture trans fats, search hydrogenated vegetable oils.

 CHEW ON THIS 3.2 If you want to avoid trans fats, don't rely just on the nutrition facts label where it lists the grams of fats. Food companies are allowed to claim their products contain 0g trans fats as long as it is >0.5g/serving. Instead, look at the ingredients and see if there are any hydrogenated or partially hydrogenated oils (there are a variety of vegetable oils that are hydrogenated).

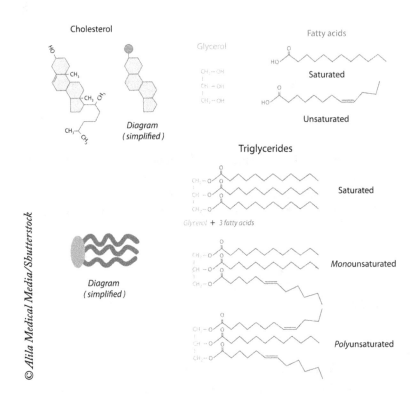

© Alila Medical Media/Shutterstock

FUNCTIONS OF FAT

There are some basic uses for fats. First and foremost, all of your cell membranes—and every organism's cell membranes—are made of two layers of a fatty substance called a phospholipid. Imagine that your cells are formed like a tennis ball or coconut. If you cut either of these in half, they are hollow inside. But instead of being surrounded by air inside and out, your cells are surrounded by water. Functionally, if the cell membrane was composed only of a fatty substance, it would clump together into a blob of fat because the water would repel the fat. So when life evolved this common barrier, any two fats (think straws) were combined with a phosphate group, which is a common substance found in every one of your cells (think of the phosphate group as a Styrofoam ball). The result of this combination is called a phospholipid (think Styrofoam ball with the two straws coming off it like a tail). Interestingly, the phosphate group loves water and, therefore, is called **hydrophilic**. But, remember, because the lipids are **hydrophobic**, they will push away the water and the water-loving substances. Therefore, the resulting phospholipid has opposing characteristics: hydrophilic/hydrophobic.

This hydrophilic/hydrophobic dichotomy is very valuable for life to exist: All cells have water inside them and are also surrounded by water, which enables the billions of phospholipids in each cell to organize themselves in a double-coating that provides a protective barrier for each cell. In both coats, the phospho-part faces the water and the lipid-part from each coat faces the inward (toward each other). (*See the diagram on page 5*). Imagine the lipids as being Velcro strips that function as a unit, are sticky and are most useful when sticking together. The cell membrane, especially these lipids, make it possible for us to maintain homeostasis and detects and responds to the outside world by being selective in what is imported and exported. Lipids are amazing and, with a little help from some friends, keep you functioning well. (TBCL—see cholesterol, proteins, transport.)

Fats play a major role in our body in terms of energy storage, insulation, and cushioning. Fats are stored in specialized cells called **adipose tissue**. Adipose is the wonderful stuff you probably refer to as cellulite. This may seem like an unwanted substance because it is associated with being overweight or obese, but you need fat stores and your body naturally wants you to have the reserve just in case you don't have access to food for a while. The fat that you consume is fashioned together into a substance called a **triglyceride**, where three fats, regardless of the type—saturated, unsaturated, or trans—are bound together for energy storage.

Triglycerides are stored within different types of fat cells: white and brown fat cells. White fat cells are just lumps of triglycerides whereas brown fat cells are dynamic fat-burning cells that continuously burn to heat up the body. The white fat cells outnumber the brown fat cells and are key for producing metabolic hormones, while the brown cells will help to burn fat within the white fat cells. Your body's fat cells are normally located below the surface of the skin, but can also be located in the abdomen or visceral region, which has been shown to be very stressful on your organs. The process of **lipolysis** is your body's way of breaking down fats in your cells to produce energy; **ketosis** is another cellular process that involves transforming a fat into sugar to restore blood sugar levels (TBCL).

 EXERCISE YOUR BRAIN 3.2 Let's explore the structure of fats. Search for images of the four different types of fats. Make a drawing of the different types, illustrating how the structural differences relate to their state in the form of solid, semi-solid or liquid at room temperature.

Take home functions:

In your cells: Fats make up the membranes of your cells and all internal compartments; they are signaling hormones; and they produce energy.

In your body: Fats store energy long-term, and provide cushioning to protect vital organs and bones. They also provide the energy to maintain body temperature (thermoregulation) and insulate the body against drastic temperature changes.

CHOLESTEROL

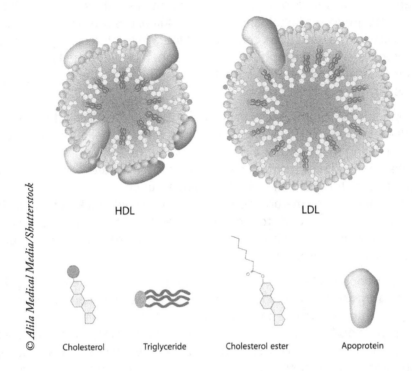

© *Alila Medical Media/Shutterstock*

HDL   LDL

Cholesterol   Triglyceride   Cholesterol ester   Apoprotein

Cholesterol is the next substance listed on the nutrition facts label. **Cholesterol** is a molecule that is universally required by all organisms; however, there are some other functions for cholesterol that are specific to humans. Most people don't think of cholesterol as a nutrient that their body requires, but rather as the stuff you get measured at the doctor's office (TBCL). But there is a fundamental difference between the molecules you read about on the food label and the complexes that are measured at the doctor's office. The cholesterol listed on the nutrition label is a measurement of the amount of the molecule in that product. The molecule of cholesterol, which is made up of rings of carbon and hydrogen, is relatively small but has very valuable functions. This substance is hydrophobic just like fats, so it isn't surprising to find out that cholesterol is a necessary component of the cell membrane.

The cell membrane is composed of many other components, with the majority being the double-coated phospholipids that we've described, but it also has a lot of cholesterol to help stabilize the membrane at varying temperatures. At high temperatures, the membrane wants to become more like a liquid, but cholesterol helps to keep those phospholipids together and remain a membrane. At low temperatures, the cholesterol molecules will push the phospholipids apart, keeping the membrane fluid. Another reason you need cholesterol is that it is the base for making Vitamin D, estrogen, testosterone and other steroid hormones. All food organisms will contain cholesterol, but certain ones, such as organ meats, eggs, and shellfish, have higher concentrations of cholesterol.

BOIL IT DOWN 3.2 If you are interested in the function of cholesterol-based substances, search for sterols and steroid hormones.

CHEW ON THIS 3.3 Cholesterol molecules that are found on the food label are not the same as the blood cholesterol that gets measured in your bloodstream. Instead, cholesterol the molecule is transported around your body along with fats within two different huge transport proteins called low density lipoprotein (**LDL**) and high density lipoprotein (**HDL**). Remember both cholesterol and fats hate water so they need a protein to transport them. (TBCL)

Take home functions:

>**In your cells:** Cholesterol helps to maintain the membranes of cells at varying temperatures, and it is the base structure to produce essential steroid signals/substances.

>**In your body:** Cholesterol the molecule is not the same substance as blood cholesterol, which causes cardiovascular issues.

SODIUM

Sodium is the next nutrient listed on a nutrition facts label and is a charged atom (called an ion) found mainly in the form of salt (which is sodium chloride). **Sodium** and other ions are necessary for your cells to transport substances and send signals to your body.

Organisms regulate the import and export of ions in different ways. The overall theme for all of life is that some ions are purposefully moved into the cell and others moved out and, at times, some that are typically moved out are allowed in. This dynamic process facilitates organisms to perform large tasks. For example, your muscle cells require positive ions to assist in the contraction of your muscles. Your body also requires these ions to generate electricity in your nervous system to send signals. Additionally, sodium affects the balance of water inside cells. Many food organisms have salt added to them for the general purpose of food preservation, which has occurred for millennia. In reality, however, all organisms—because they require sodium for their own survival—already have this ion in them. The nutritional issue with sodium is that consuming high levels of added salt can cause pressure on our cells and specifically puts demand on the circulatory system, which is very harmful over the long-term.

 BOIL IT DOWN 3.3 If you are interested in what types of ions are used in your body and what their functions are, search biologically functional ions.

Take home functions:

>**In your cells:** Sodium helps to maintain homeostasis of external and internal differences in ion concentrations of all cells.

>**In your body:** Sodium can assist in propagating messages for the nervous system, such as the contraction of muscles and maintaining water balance.

CARBOHYDRATES

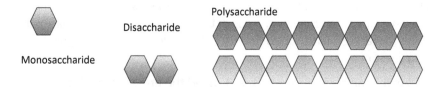

Basic Structure of Carbohydrates

Carbohydrates are the next category of nutrients that you will encounter on the nutrition facts label. Basically, carbs are nutrients that your body uses for energy. This molecule is composed of carbon, oxygen, and hydrogen in small rings. When the ring stands alone, it's known as **monosaccharides**; when linked in pairs, they are called **disaccharides**; and if there are a lot of rings that are bound together in very large molecules, they are called **polysaccharides**. Polysaccharides fall into a category of large molecules (aka macromolecules) called **polymers**. You may think of carbs as being sugars: Technically, sugars are carbs, but not all carbs are sugars. Sugars are a subcategory of carbs, which includes all monosaccharides and disaccharides. Your body requires both monosaccharides and polysaccharides.

 BOIL IT DOWN 3.4 If you are interested in exploring the shape of sugars and carbs, search images of monosaccharides, disaccharides, and polysaccharides.

SUGAR

The monosaccharides that you encounter most frequently are **glucose** and **fructose**. Disaccharides result when two of these smaller sugars are linked together, with the most common form being sucrose, also known as table sugar, which is a combination of glucose and fructose. If you can visualize sugar in the form that you sometimes encounter it—as syrup or honey—it will help you remember one of its major functions: being sticky. Hence sugar helps cells stick together.

Sugar's most important role is that it provides your body with energy. Because your body is so large (no offense!) and is made up of so many cells that require energy throughout the various levels of activities, you need to be able to store the monosaccharides for when you need the energy. The monosaccharides are fashioned into the polysaccharide **glycogen**. Glycogen is stored mainly in your muscles and liver. We will discuss how we tap into this energy source later. Just like us, other organisms universally use monosaccharides to generate energy to live. Because of this, we find carbs in every food organism.

Fruits have a high concentration of sugars because their evolutionary purpose is to attract a seed-dispersing animal. Honey's very high sugar concentration is due to the nectar collected from flowers and its subsequent concentration of that liquid is a food source for the beehive. In addition to naturally occurring sugars, we also have industrial processes to extract and/or concentrate sugars into different forms.

 EXERCISE YOUR BRAIN 3.3 Ingredients don't have to be universal in how they are listed, and this is sometimes a way companies can "sneak" in added sugar. Find a list of different ways glucose, fructose, sucrose and other sugars can be listed under ingredients. Hint: There are at least 35 ways added sugar can be listed.

COMPLEX CARBOHYDRATES

The complex carbs are definitely found in many of the foods you eat. There is a plant polysaccharide called **starch**, which is similar to glycogen in animals. Hence, it is a reserve for stored energy. There are two locations within plants that you will find starch: either in portions of an existing plant or in the seed/grain. In an existing plant, the starch is produced mainly in areas of the plant that are responsible for regrowth such as bulbs (onions) or tubers (potatoes). These are below-ground structures that will give rebirth to the plant during the next growing season.

Starch can also be found within an area of a grain (seed) called the endosperm. Whole grains are valuable because of the variety of nutrients they contain. Since the point of the grain is to produce a new plant it must have all the nutrients needed for life. There are three main structures of a grain. The external protective shell called the bran contains lots of fiber (see below). Internally there is the large endosperm where reserve energy is located in the form of starch and proteins (this is where the gluten proteins are located). These supply the third structure called the germ, which is the baby plant with the energy to grow into a new plant.

 CHEW ON THIS 3.4 Flour is made by extracting just the endosperm of a grain and grinding up this material into a powder.

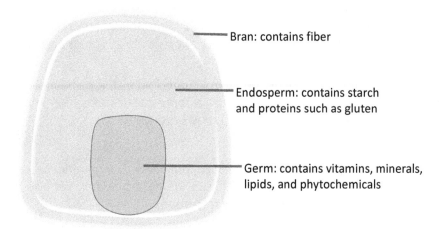

Bran: contains fiber

Endosperm: contains starch and proteins such as gluten

Germ: contains vitamins, minerals, lipids, and phytochemicals

FIBER

Another complex carbohydrate subcategory is called fiber. There are many different carbohydrates that fall into the category of fiber, but the most common is called **cellulose. Fiber** is a carb that plants produce and deposit in their **cell walls** to make the cell rigid, which gives these cells enough strength to grow tall. Another very strong polysaccharide you encounter, though not as frequently, is chitin, the strong sugar that makes up exoskeletons of many invertebrates. All plants and vegetables have fiber, but leafy greens, beans, and the whole grains—such as corn, rice, quinoa, bulgur, and whole wheat—contain larger amounts (TBCL).

Take home functions:

In your cells: Carbohydrates provide energy, store energy, and make your cells sticky.

In your body: Carbohydrates that can't be digested (aka fiber) reduce absorption of other nutrients, cleanse the digestive tract, and make you feel more satiated for a longer period of time.

 CHEW ON THIS 3.5 Cellulose is not only the most common carbohydrate, but it is also the most common organic molecule on earth because not many organisms have the ability to break down its complex structure.

PROTEINS

Proteins are the last item within the main area of the nutrition fact label. Proteins are what make you appear and act unique. They make you, you! This does not, however, diminish the importance of the other substances we have discussed because life wouldn't persist without each of those other substances.

Proteins also fall into the category of polymers. Their ingredients (monomers) are called **amino acids**. You will hear about these if you go to a supplement store. Amino acids come in many forms; specifically, 20 different types exist, and for most of your life you cannot manufacture eight of these types, which is why they are considered essential. The other 12 are nonessential because you can make them from other substances you consume. Your cells can take these ingredients and combine them together in many different ways and sequences to make a useful protein or a non-useful protein.

The sequence of amino acids determines the structure of the protein, which defines the shape of the protein. The shape of the protein determines how it functions in your body. Even one mistake in the sequence can make these proteins work or fail miserably resulting in a nonfunctional protein. These non-functional or abnormal proteins can cause devastating disease such as cystic fibrosis or (as a happy accident) enable you to be HIV resistant.

BOIL IT DOWN 3.5 If you are interested in finding out more about foods high in proteins, search for protein-rich foods (don't get fooled by claims on food products!).

CHEW ON THIS 3.6 Plastic Tupperware™ containers are polymers. Any generic macromolecule formed by combining smaller units called monomers is considered a polymer. We also will discuss other polymers, such as proteins, nucleic acids, and hydrocarbons.

FUNCTIONS OF PROTEINS

Once again, just like fats and carbs, proteins are not just ingested and ready to go. Instead, their ingredients—the amino acids—are absorbed and you manufacture your own proteins based upon information within your DNA and instruction from your body on when to produce these proteins and where they are needed. What function do proteins perform in your body? A very cool function of proteins is that they allow you to have color—skin, eye and hair color. They also allow you to transport things such as the fatty protein complexes LDL and HDL, which we likened to buses that carry fats around your body (TBCL). Another amazing feature of proteins is that they are signals. Proteins can be released as signals from a cell, stay within the cell or be embedded in the cell membrane. A good example of a protein signal is insulin. You will explore insulin more later (TBCL), but interestingly insulin cannot do its job unless the cell contains another protein within its cell membrane called a receptor (it receives the message). Additionally, in the cell membrane, proteins are importers and exporters. We know that the fats of the membrane keep most things out. Well, proteins in the membrane fall into one of two categories of "helpers"—either they are tunnels (called **channel proteins**) or they are transporters (called **carrier proteins**) to get a substance in and out of the cell past the impenetrable barrier of fat. Proteins in the membrane enable cells to latch together forming tissues, which, over evolutionary time, allowed for larger organisms to exist. Because larger organisms could make tissues that then were able to build organs into organ systems, complex multicellular organisms evolved. You are one of these complex organisms, so thank your proteins!

BOIL IT DOWN 3.6 If you interested in the intricate structure of proteins, search primary, secondary, tertiary, and quaternary structure of proteins/polypeptides.

EXERCISE YOUR BRAIN 3.4 We have now discussed at least three components of your cell membrane. Make a list of all the components that make up a typical cell membrane and give their functions.

CHEW ON THIS 3.7 It's weird to think that DNA produces protein, but also requires proteins to produce them.

Another job that proteins are in charge of is defense. Using many different methods, they defend you from bleeding out, or from being invaded by different types of microbes and to remember those pathogens to fight against them in the future. Proteins make your system functional because the DNA code needs help to function and proteins are ready to pitch in and make the DNA work. Finally, the most relevant function to your digestion is that proteins help speed up reactions; these type of proteins are called **enzymes** (TBCL). Without enzymes, large organisms (like us) would not exist because we wouldn't be able to extract enough from our food without enzymes. Don't be fooled though, because even bacteria and other microbes require enzymes!

So where do you find these amazing nutrients? Most people equate proteins with meat, which is correct. For muscle (protein!) to be functional, it requires a lot of proteins to be located within the cells. Therefore, when you consume meat in any form, you are consuming a lot of proteins. But meat is not the only place you will encounter protein; beans and nuts, for example, also have a high content of this nutrient. Additionally, protein can be obtained in small amounts from grassy grains, specifically in the endosperm; where there's a high content of starch, there is also protein.

Take home functions:

In your cells: Proteins are structural, provide transport, are catalytic, provide communication, and regulate genes.

In your body: Proteins store energy, transport substances around the body, and impart different physical characteristics such as skin, eye and hair color, everything!

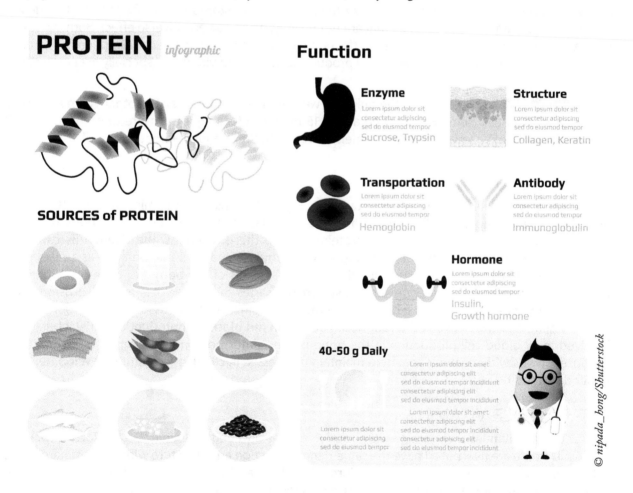

© nipada_hong/Shutterstock

VITAMINS

This can be a confusing category because many people mistakenly believe that they should consume as much of these nutrients as possible. **Vitamins** are small organic substances that your body requires to function. One of the great things about vitamins is that they don't need to be broken down to be absorbed; they are small enough to come across the cell membrane on their own. Your cells require each different type of vitamin for a different reason.

There are two classes of vitamins divided by whether they love water (hydrophilic) or hate water (hydrophobic): They are called water soluble and fat soluble vitamins. **Water soluble vitamins** can be absorbed into your system, utilized where they're needed and then excreted. **Fat soluble vitamins** can easily get into your system, but they are stored in your fat (adipose) tissue and, therefore, these can build up to levels that are not healthy, having a very adverse effect. Both classes can be over-consumed and both have adverse effects at high and low levels. Over-consumption of vitamins is mainly due to eating supplements and food products fortified with vitamins, especially in energy drinks.

 CHEW ON THIS 3.8 Vitamin D is the only one we can manufacture so all the other vitamins are considered essential. Humans only need about 15 minutes of sunlight exposure to produce the daily requirement of Vitamin D, but most Americans don't get this requisite amount of sunlight.

WATER-SOLUBLE VITAMINS

Water-soluble vitamins include all eight Vitamin Bs. Many of the Bs (B1—thiamine, B2—riboflavin, B3—niacin, B5—pantothenic acid, B7—biotin, and B12—cobalamin) are involved in your body producing energy from carbohydrates, fats and/or proteins. During these reactions, the Vitamin Bs can act as cofactors, which means that they either help your enzymes speed up a reaction, act as a reactant, or as an enzyme. Others have very specific roles in other systems of the body. For example, Vitamin B6 (pyridoxine) is a cofactor to generate nervous system messages. B9 (folic acid) aids in cell division during development, for example when a baby is generating its spinal cord and tissues that surround it, folic acid is required, and it is involved throughout your life in red blood cell production. B12 (cobalamin) is involved in all blood cell production in the bone marrow. Your body needs Vitamin C (ascorbic acid) because it helps with reactions that help maintain cells, assist in cell division during development, and repair damaged tissues.

FAT-SOLUBLE VITAMINS

The fat-soluble vitamins are Vitamins A, D, E, and K. You mainly need Vitamin A (beta-carotene) for vision. Vitamin D (there are five, but all have the same general function and structure with the root name called calciferol) facilitates the absorption of calcium, phosphate and other minerals that you use for bone growth and repair. Vitamin E (tocopherol) aids in maintaining your cell membranes as well as having a role in producing red blood cells. Vitamin K is found in both natural forms (with the root name of quinone) and man-made forms. This vitamin is necessary in blood clotting, clearing of bruising/damage, and maintenance of bones and tissues.

Many vitamins have dual functions, such as those that are considered **antioxidants**. Vitamins A, C, and E, along with other substances, either natural or man-made, can sequester free radicals, which are damaging products of cellular reactions. Other vitamins, A, B6, B9, B12, D and E, assist in strengthening your immune system's responses.

Vitamins conveniently show us where they are! Any colored fruit or vegetable has vitamins. Dark leafy greens have most nutrients you require, and definitely provide an amazing mixture of vitamins.

Take home functions:

In your cells: Vitamins maintain many different types of cells and tissues, assist in energy (ATP) production, and remove harmful substances from your cells.

In your body: Vitamins guide tissue and organ development, help you see, repair damage to your blood vessels, aid in the production of cells, and assist your immune system.

 EXERCISE YOUR BRAIN 3.5 List all the vitamins in a table, their function and find a specific food organism that has a lot of that vitamin.

MINERALS

Most **minerals** are readily found within our diet. Much like vitamins, many minerals have dual functions. One of the most common functions is cellular homeostasis (chlorine, phosphorus, potassium, and sodium) and signaling for nervous and muscular function (calcium, chlorine, and sodium). Many of these minerals are found as ions that perform these functions. Minerals are a part of crucial substances such as proteins (copper, iodine, iron, magnesium, manganese, molybdenum, sulfur, and zinc) or vitamins (cobalt and selenium). They help maintain your tissues, such as your teeth and bones (calcium, fluorine, and phosphorus). They also can assist in breaking down our food/substances to extract energy (chlorine, chromium, iron, and zinc).

All minerals are required in very small portions, but an imbalance can have devastating effects on your health. Iron deficiency, which leads to a type of anemia, is very common. Why do you need iron? Iron is necessary at very low levels for transporting oxygen. Since all your cells require oxygen, your body requires iron in your diet. Iodine assists your thyroid gland—located in your throat—to operate correctly. With low levels of iodine, the thyroid gland will take on fluid and grow into a goiter (some goiters are also caused by other reasons, such as genetics). Fluorine helps your mouth to combat against pathogenic bacteria and maintain healthy teeth.

Take home functions:

In your cells: Minerals maintain cell homeostasis, nourish your cells, and assist in energy production.

In your body: Minerals are critical in the function of your nervous system, and play a crucial role in transport of gases, your immune responses, and metabolism.

 EXERCISE YOUR BRAIN 3.6 List all the minerals required in your diet and describe their function.

Overall, the food label is a guide to the nutrients you require and those you should look to limit, but now let's see how these nutrients can be manipulated during food production and then how your body retrieves these nutrients from whatever food you consume.

 CHEW ON THIS 3.9 Ingredients on a food product label are listed from the largest to smallest amount.

EXERCISE YOUR BRAIN 3.7 Make a list of the nutrients we have discussed. Find at least two websites—use one government and one private website—and compare their recommended daily values for these nutrients. Explain why there are differences or similarities between these recommendations.

 BOIL IT DOWN 3.7 If you are interested in daily values that have recently changed, search for new recommendations for daily values.

GET THE SKINNY

Adipose Tissue—where fats are stored for reserves, sometimes called cellulite.

Amino Acids—basic units that can be reused by your body to make proteins and other substances to build and support your tissues such as muscles, bones, blood, and other body organs.

Antioxidants—a substance that binds free radicals produced in cellular reactions that can damage your cells/body.

Carbohydrates—any monosaccharide, disaccharide, or polysaccharide. Your body breaks these down to produce energy.

Carrier Proteins—located in the cell membrane, they are transporters of substances into the cell.

Cell Wall—a barrier in cells that regulates what goes in or comes out of the cell and also gives the cell rigidity.

Cellulose—the main type of fiber, it is a polysaccharide of glucose that constitutes the chief part of the cell walls of plants.

Channel Proteins—located in the cell membrane, they act as tunnels for substances to get past the fats.

Cholesterol—a hydrophobic molecule used to build cell walls, to make vitamin D and some hormones, and create bile salts that help you digest fat.

Disaccharides—a disaccharide is a carbohydrate that is formed when two monosaccharides are joined together such as table sugar.

Enzymes—proteins that speed up reactions, such as digestion.

Essential Nutrients—any nutrient an organism requires but is unable to make itself.

Fat-Soluble—any substance which is hydrophobic and is typically stored in your adipose tissue.

Fiber—carbohydrates that can't be digested. It's in the plants we eat for food: fruits, vegetables, grains, and legumes.

Gluten—combination of two proteins, found in the endosperm of grains.

Glycogen—whereas glucose is the main source of fuel for our cells, glycogen is the stored form of glucose, primarily in your liver or muscles.

HDL—high density lipoprotein known as "good cholesterol" because it clears LDL out of arteries and returns fats and cholesterol to their storage cells.

Hydrogenation—a process whereby an unsaturated fat gets treated with hydrogen, converting it to the same structure as a saturated fat.

Hydrophilic—means "water-loving," and it describes the ability to mix/interact between water and substances, such as proteins and salts.

Hydrophobic—means "water-fearing," and it describes the segregation and repulsion between water and substances, such as fats.

Ketosis—process whereby your body converts fat into products that can be used to burn for energy.

LDL—low density lipoprotein known as "bad" cholesterol because it can clog arteries. Delivers fats and cholesterol to your cells.

Lipolysis—general breakdown of fats

Minerals—a substance that is normally found in salt form or a free element required in your body in very small amounts to function properly.

Non-essential Nutrients—nutrients that your body requires but that your cells are able to manufacture enough of on its own.

Nucleotide—a monomer of DNA and RNA.

Polymers—"mer" means "part," so polymers are substances made of many parts and monomers are made of one part.

Proteins—polymers of amino acids that make you, you! Proteins build, maintain, and replace the tissues in your body.

Saturated Fats—fat that's solid at room temperature and typically comes from animal sources and at high levels can elevate blood cholesterol.

Sodium—a charged atom, mainly found in the form of salt, that helps transport substances throughout your body and move substances in and out of your cells.

Starch—is similar to glycogen, but comes from plant cells. Starch is an end product of photosynthesis and serves as the chemical storage form of energy.

Trans Fat—"bad fat" is solid or semi-solid at room temperature, is made from oils (good fats) through a food processing method called hydrogenation.

Triglyceride—three fats bound together for energy storage.

Unsaturated Fats—"good fat" is liquid at room temperature, comes from a plant, such as olive oil and have been shown to decrease blood cholesterol levels. Comes in two types: monounsaturated (nuts & plant oils) and polyunsaturated (essential fatty acids, i.e., omega 3s).

Vitamins—essential organic molecules used in energy production, maintenance of tissues, immune response, vision, and metabolic reactions.

Water-Soluble—any substance which is hydrophilic and can be excreted but at repeated high levels will challenge you kidneys to excrete it.

Section 4
HOW DOES YOUR FOOD GET FROM YOUR MOUTH TO YOUR DERRIERE?

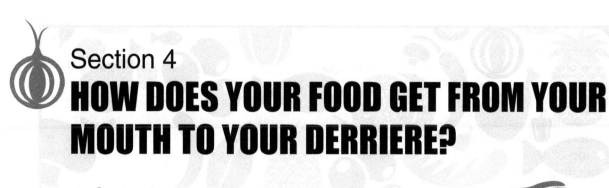

Food Production, Enzymes and Reactions, and Digestion

Food Production

FOOD FOR THOUGHT

Let's focus on some topics that are in the news: GMOs, preservatives, additives, stabilizers, dyes. As you probably now understand, knowing where your food comes from and how the ingredients are used by your body is essential to your ability to make decisions about your diet and health. Additionally, consuming a diet that is well balanced, rich in nutrients and consists mainly of your naturally occurring fellow organisms is clearly a wise approach to your nutrition. So, how do all these nutrition buzzwords affect you and your diet? And why is there such a backlash against processed foods?

The bottom line is that the extensive preparation and processing of foods—which may, in fact, enhance the colors, augment the flavors, extend the shelf lives, improve the texture, or reduce the calories—has adverse effects, such as:

- diminished nutrients,
- corrupted benefits,
- new health risks because of altered chemicals,
- additional empty calories, and
- interference with our body's natural relationship with other organisms.

GENETICALLY MODIFIED ORGANISMS

A **GMO**, which stands for a genetically modified organism, is made by inserting new DNA into an existing organism. Although the name GMO is commonly used to refer to this process of genetically manipulating a bacterium, fungus, plant, or animal in the laboratory to use in food production, it is not truly an accurate name. Technically, humans have been genetically modifying organisms for food and for pets by selecting for beneficial or desirable characteristics for eons. A more appropriate name would be a genetically engineered organism, meaning a laboratory technique was used to create something new in the organisms by inserting DNA to affect the outcome. Normally, the new DNA is from a completely different species, and is added because the new DNA adds a beneficial piece of DNA to the organism. There are different applications for this process; for example, pharmaceutical companies use GMOs to manufacture drugs such as insulin. Doctors might use GMOs for gene therapy, which is where a person with a genetic disease receives an injection with the corrected gene. The application for GMOs that has been dominating the news is how they are utilized within our food. Bacteria, plants, fungi, and animals can all be genetically modified within our food. These include the bacteria used in yogurts, yeast used in production of wine, beer, and cheese, and even farm-raised animals, which are modified to grow faster so that they can be sold faster.

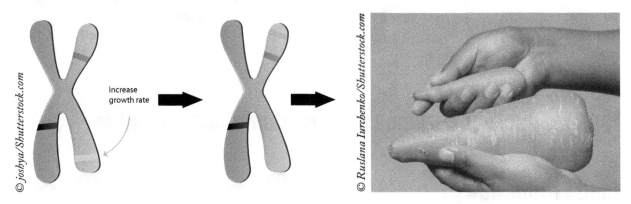

The most common type of GMOs used in your food or in food production are plants. You don't typically eat most GMO plants; instead, the most common GMO crops such as wheat and corn are produced to feed animals such as cows, pigs, and chickens. Soybeans are another commonly modified crop; they are primarily used for animal feed, but in your food, they are mainly processed to extract the different substances they contain, such as soy lecithin, oil, and the other traditional soy foods such as soy sauce, tofu, and soy milk.

 BOIL IT DOWN 4.1 If you interested in understanding the types of GMOs, search types of GMOs used in food production.

Why are there so many more plants than animals being genetically modified? Well, plants are much easier to manipulate, and they are also extremely important because they are the base of your food web. In modifying plants, we can adjust so many different characteristics that can allow food to be produced at a faster pace and contain more nutrients, as well as become less susceptible to disease, and stronger than the plants that surround them.

Many plants are modified to produce a natural pesticide to protect them against pests—for example, the toxin Bacillus thuringiensis. Plants can even be modified to be resistant to herbicides such as RoundUp™, which allows farmers to treat a field with an herbicide to kill any plants that are competing with the crop for water and other nutrients.

Currently the United States doesn't require any indication on the food label that the food product contains GMOs, but there is a movement from organic farmers to indicate that their products do not contain GMOs.

WHAT IS PROCESSED FOOD?

Food processing manipulates the original organism in a way that extracts nutrients from it. This is a very broad definition, but relates to how we should approach and understand what's in the food products we consume. The main types of additives used in food processing target the characteristics of flavor, shelf life, consistency, color, and nutritional content.

Companies add many different substances to products that increase shelf life by decreasing the likelihood of microbes growing. These substances, of course, are considered preservatives. Preservatives assist in preventing microbes from growing mainly by making the conditions inhospitable. We have discussed preservatives, but those were in the context of preserving foods that aren't usually processed. Often, preservation depends on the type of food that is being preserved and which preservative technique is used. For example, if it's canned fruits and vegetables, then salt, calcium chloride, or citric acid might be used, whereas processed meats and fish might be preserved with phosphates/sodium nitrate/nitrite.

Flavor enhancers increase a certain aspect of taste, for example, hydrolyzed protein increases the "meaty" or umami taste. Stabilizers are used to keep the consistency of the food product from changing while it waits on the shelf to be purchased. This will also depend on the type of food, whether it is a dried food or canned or if it is a liquid, solid, or semisolid. Like preservatives, some of these are natural substances extracted from other organisms such as carrageenan, which is found in seaweed.

Lastly, there are food dyes, which can be natural such as beet juice, or synthetic like red dye #9. For instance, a farmed raised salmon don't have a pink color because it's not eating the natural krill shrimp that makes it pink, so a dye is used to color the salmon to make it more appealing to customers. You will find any of these additives listed in the ingredients list on the food label. Do you know how your body processes the dyes, and furthermore, do you think there are nutritional benefits to consuming these dyes? It's worth considering.

What's all the fuss about processed sugars such as high fructose corn syrup? Typically, naturally occurring sucrose/starch from a plant such as corn can be broken down into glucose or a combination of glucose and fructose where the glucose can then be converted into fructose. When it's further processed to form a sugar such as high fructose corn syrup, the fructose is concentrated to be anywhere from 40–90% of the sugar. So why do companies use this process? Because humans perceive fructose to be a sweeter substance than glucose or sucrose, so it allows companies to make highly-sweetened products for a cheap price!

One last attribute manufacturers can manipulate is the addition of "good" nutrients to enhance the nutritional value of either a processed or natural food to make it more nutritionally valuable and/or appealing to the consumer. Fortification is the process of adding minerals and vitamins to the food such as Vitamin D or iron, the deficit of which which often are the cause of malnourishment in the population.

 BOIL IT DOWN 4.2 If you are interested in other food product claims, search heart healthy, light, low sodium, low fat, all-natural, and cage-free.

UNDERSTANDING FOOD LABELS

Food products can also have health or production claims that may sometimes be confusing. For example, do you know the differences between foods labeled as "organic" versus those labeled "natural"? **Organic** is anything that isn't a GMO, hasn't been treated with pesticides, herbicides, hormones, or antibiotics; has been raised in manner that reflects how the organism would live in nature; and helps to maintain or increase the biodiversity of the area. Organic food production reflects an attitude of respecting the organisms that not only are used to produce food for us, but to try to do it with as little impact on other organisms that exist around us as well.

"Natural," on the other hand, is more an indication of what's in a food product. Foods labeled as "**natural**" are not highly processed, and don't have synthetic additives such as preservatives, sweeteners, oils, stabilizers, emulsifiers, or growth hormones. Why is this important? Well, many of the chemicals and additives that are used to prepare food for its time in the package and leading up to its consumption are not healthy and, in many cases are harmful to our bodies. If you are choosing to eliminate harmful chemicals from your diet, then you look for foods labeled "natural."

FOOD PREPARATION

The nutritional value of a food can be altered by the way it's prepared. There are countless methods for cooking food: pan searing in butter or oil, boiling, baking, frying, grilling, and smoking all can change the nutritional characteristics of food. All methods, except in the case of cold smoking, primarily change food by heating it to varying degrees.

Heat, as we know, is energy and we measure this energy with a thermometer that indicates to you how fast the molecules are moving. Heating is a very useful tool, as is illustrated in your own body when you get a fever to fight off an infection by bursting open the microbe's cells. Well, we use heat during cooking to stimulate substances within our food to react. As heat increases, so does the movement of molecules, which will both break things down and build things up as well as change the characteristics of substances such as proteins. Heat causes proteins to unfold from their three-dimensional shape in a process called denaturation, which is similar to what the acid in your stomach does to open up the protein so the enzymes can chew at it. By changing the shape, the texture of the food becomes different. Think of an egg, which has lots of protein in the egg white. When you crack an egg open, the egg white isn't really white at all. Instead, it is clear because the egg protein albumin is still intact, but as soon as you apply heat to the egg white, it is no longer clear and no longer a liquid. The proteins unfold and bind together forming a semi-solid substance.

Cooking the food will essentially start to predigest it and prepare nutrients for digestion in your body. Some nutrients can be lost during the cooking process; for example, boiling can cause some water-soluble to leak out of the food. Other times, the cooking process actually facilitates the creation of new substances; when your meat or certain vegetables burn on the grill, carcinogens are formed! But our bodies deal with food—whether it is processed or not—in generally the same manner: it enters the digestive tract and encounters the harsh environment that will ultimately break it apart, mainly by the group of proteins called enzymes.

 BOIL IT DOWN 4.3 If you are interested in finding out more about what can interfere with enzyme function, search competitive and noncompetitive inhibitors.

Enzymes and Reactions

FOOD FOR THOUGHT

Both the production and digestion of food in your body center around a specialized type of reaction that involves a catalytic protein called an **enzyme.** In the grand scheme of things, enzymes are important for you to understand because they allow you to digest food, to make all the necessary large substances your body needs—such as the protein that makes your hair brown and your eyes blue, or the energy you need to simply move a muscle! How cool are enzymes? So, the reason you need to know about enzymes is that they enable you to be you and function at every level.

HOW REACTIONS WORK

All of the important reactions that occur in your body would happen naturally, but enzymes are what make them happen way faster and way more efficiently. Reactions are about the correct position and the right amount of energy and can occur naturally by reactants hitting one another in the correct spot to form a product (think of putting the circle peg in the circle hole). Another way reactions occur is when the energy within the area—mainly in the form of heat energy—provides the energy required to break apart a reactant into smaller products or even build a larger substance from smaller ingredients.

All reactions involve the simple formula of what goes in (reactant(s)) is different from what comes out (product(s)). In an enzymatic reaction, the reactants are given a specific title: **substrate**. Most reactions require an input of energy. The level of energy, which is called **activation energy**, is different depending on what the reaction is trying to achieve. The activation energy determines how long it will take for the reaction to occur, which is also known as the **rate of reaction**. In order for life to become as large and complicated as it is today, it had to evolve a method for dealing with the limitation of the rate of reactions that are necessary for supporting more complex beings. Eventually, a mutation led to a protein (an enzyme) that could speed up a rate of reaction. Since it helped the organism that evolved this mutation, the mutation persisted in the population. More and more enzymes were eventually produced, allowing more reactions to occur at a faster pace. Now, all organisms produce a slew of different enzymes that allow them to function effectively in their given environment.

The Lock and Key Mechanism

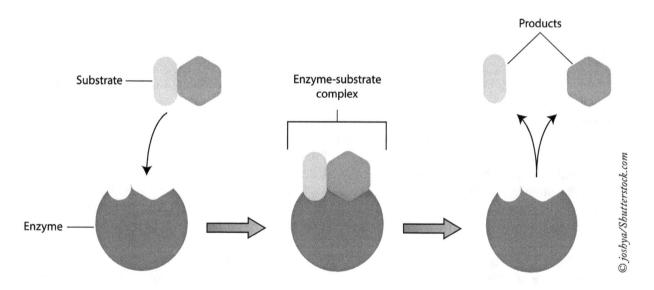

© joshya/Shutterstock.com

Enzymes work only if they have a three-dimensional structure with a specific area called an **active site**. The active site is the reaction area of the enzyme, which can surround the substrate(s). Upon surrounding the substrate(s), the enzyme positions the substrate(s) in the perfect spot to reduce the amount of activation energy, allowing the reaction to occur at an astronomically faster pace.

 EXERCISE YOUR BRAIN 4.1 Come up with an analogy about enzymatic reactions related to humans: Who is/are the reactant(s)? Who is the enzyme? Who is/are the product(s)?

Enzymatic Reactions

FOOD FOR THOUGHT

Two different types of enzymatic reactions exist: catabolic and anabolic reactions. These determine what the product will be in size and potential/kinetic energy. **Catabolic reaction**s are those that breakdown a substance into smaller ingredients normally to release energy in the form of ATP. Since they are releasing energy from a stored source, these reactions are referred to as **exergonic. Anabolic reactions** occur when two or more reactants are brought together to form a bigger substance (think how anabolic steroids make bigger muscles). Extra energy is normally required for these, which means it will require both an enzyme and energy donated by ATP. Since these reactions require energy, they are referred to as **endergonic**.

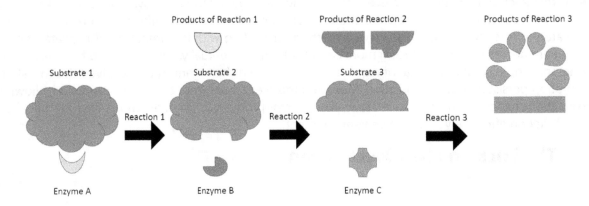

Many of these reactions are not just one step; instead the end result is brought about by a series of enzymes that work one after another to lead to the final product. This is called a **metabolic pathway**. Think of this as being similar to a cafeteria. You are supposed to start at the beginning by picking up your tray, plate, and utensils. Then, you move on to the food, then you check out and then you sit down and eat. You can't check out if you don't have food, and you can't eat if you don't have utensils. The same is true for metabolic reactions: substrate 1 has to have enzyme 1 to become substrate 2, which now will require not enzyme 1 but instead enzyme 2 to then become substrate 3 and so on until the final product is reached. For example, when the metabolic pathway produces ATP, there are actually 50 some odd different reactions in different areas of the cell based on where the enzymes are located, and each reaction is necessary for the next reaction to occur. If any given enzyme is absent or not functioning, there will be a log jam and ATP will not be produced. Although each of the 50+ reactions is unique and uses unique enzymes, the result of each reaction is the same: the production of ATP. You will see this concept at work when we discuss aerobic cellular respiration.

 BOIL IT DOWN 4.4 If you are interested in finding out more about the difference between the two types of reactions, search endergonic and exergonic enzymatic reactions.

 EXERCISE YOUR BRAIN 4.2 Describe how catabolic and anabolic reactions are related to potential and kinetic energy.

 EXERCISE YOUR BRAIN 4.3 Think of the substances we have discussed thus far and give two examples of a big substance that can be produced by an anabolic reaction and the reactants that are used to produce them.

Digestion

FOOD FOR THOUGHT

It is important for you to understand how your body uses the organisms you consume. To understand this, you must understand that, of course, your body needs to take the food and break it down to extract and absorb the many nutrients you require (and a whole bunch you don't). Now, we will explore digestion in your body. The term *digestion* is used as a catch-all name for a process that really involves ingestion, digestion, absorption, and elimination.

The Digestive System

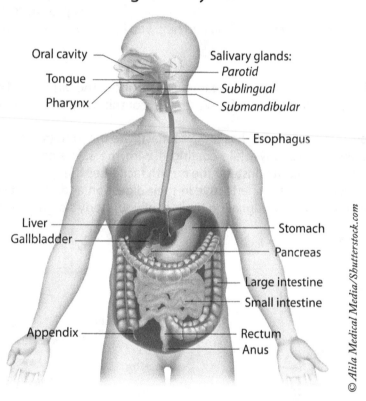

Oral cavity
Tongue
Pharynx
Salivary glands:
Parotid
Sublingual
Submandibular
Esophagus
Liver
Gallbladder
Stomach
Pancreas
Large intestine
Small intestine
Appendix
Rectum
Anus

© Alila Medical Media/Shutterstock.com

THE DIGESTIVE PROCESS: IT STARTS WITH YOUR MOUTH

As soon as food enters your mouth, it is considered to be in the digestive tract. This first step, whereby you put food into your mouth, is called ingestion. Digestion and absorption occur in several structures of your digestive tract. Normally, what is being digested in the specific part of your digestive tract is what is also being absorbed there. For example, you digest proteins in your stomach and absorb amino acids through the cells in your stomach. **Digestion** involves the presence of specific enzymes that take apart large substances to make them manageable for your body to absorb. It seems a little ridiculous, but other organisms manufacture the same types of nutrients—and sometimes the exact same protein or fat or carb—that your body needs, but these are far too large to cross over your cell membrane and must first be torn apart by the enzymatic reactions called hydrolysis. **Hydrolysis** is another aptly named process. (This doesn't happen all that often, so when scientists name a process, structure, or substance that makes sense, we like to point it out!) "Hydro" refers to water and "lysis" refers to breaking apart. The enzymatic reactions that break down the macromolecules (proteins, carbohydrates and fats) in your food add water to tear each of the subunits off of the larger molecule. This processing step makes it feasible for your system to absorb these nutrients.

BOIL IT DOWN 4.5 If you are interesting in learning more about the taste buds, search for location and concentration of taste buds.

 CHEW ON THIS 4.1 When you are sick and congested, too much mucus production in your nostrils makes it difficult for you to "taste" food and the flavor will seem abnormal.

Although the sense of taste and smell involve a chemical interaction, the actual substances detected are not broken down during the process, so consider this as a physical aspect of digestion versus a chemical one. The tongue also has taste buds that detect sweet, salty, bitter, sour, and umami (meaty flavor). Taste buds are truly important in telling your body what enzymes to produce in the rest of the system in order to appropriately digest and absorb the nutrients contained within the food you are eating. You might not think of it this way, but a key factor in your body's digestive system is your nose. It contains millions of tiny hairs that detect chemicals within your food and help you to prepare your system for what's about to come down the pipe.

 BOIL IT DOWN 4.6 If you are interested in learning more about the difference between the flavors of food versus your sense of taste, search for senses that contribute to the perception of flavor.

From a physical perspective, your mouth has teeth to masticate the food (mush it up), and your tongue will move the food around physically while coating it with the saliva containing **amylase**. Not too much absorption occurs in the mouth, instead the mouth facilitates the gathering of information that's passed along to the larger organs to be effective in their digestion and absorption. Think of it as your nose and mouth doing the recon and signaling the rest of your body's organs and systems so they can react appropriately.

Swallowing

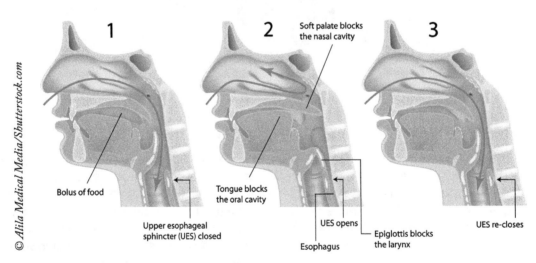

© Alila Medical Media/Shutterstock.com

1 Bolus of food — Upper esophageal sphincter (UES) closed

2 Soft palate blocks the nasal cavity — Tongue blocks the oral cavity — UES opens — Esophagus — Epiglottis blocks the larynx

3 UES re-closes

YOUR ESOPHAGUS

From your mouth, the food passes through the throat (called the pharynx) through a round muscle called the upper esophageal sphincter (UES) into the esophagus. The sphincter allows the **esophagus**, which is a long tube, to be completely shut off from the throat. The esophagus mainly acts as a transport tube and doesn't contribute to any chemical or physical processing of the food, but it does do something pretty amazing. Your esophagus is surrounded by smooth muscle (involuntary muscle), which contracts in a wave-like motion called **peristalsis**. This contraction starts from the top of the esophagus at the **UES** and will move the food as it contracts one-way towards the stomach where there resides another sphincter called the **lower esophageal sphincter** (LES). So, even if you stand on your head after swallowing food, the food will still reach your stomach and not come back up. This awesome feat is helped along by the two sphincters that are located at the top, the UES, to prevent backflow into the throat and also at the base of the esophagus above the stomach, the LES, to prevent the food and acid from moving from the stomach back into the esophagus.

 CHEW ON THIS 4.2 Your respiratory system must shut off its tube called the trachea by clamping down the **epiglottis**, preventing food from entering the wrong tube.

 CHEW ON THIS 4.3 Acid reflux occurs because the lower esophageal sphincter doesn't close properly allowing stomach acid into the esophagus. Ouch, that burns!

YOUR STOMACH

Next up on your digestive tract is your stomach. Physically, your **stomach** is a stretchable sac that has folds called **rugae**, which contract to effectively churn the food around. Your stomach is actually a very dangerous environment even for your cells. The stomach fluid contains a substance called **hydrochloric acid (HCl)**. This acid would dissolve most of your cells upon contact, but because your body is an amazing machine, your stomach also produces mucus that protects the cells contained in it. The purpose of the HCl acid is to unwind the three-dimensional structure of proteins so that it is open to be broken down. Meanwhile, there is also an enzyme produced by the stomach called pepsin. **Pepsin** is responsible for beginning the process of breaking apart the amino acids of the proteins. It can only do this if the protein is opened up for the enzyme to go to work. Therefore, the physical act of churning around the food by the rugae is important because it enables the food to be constantly coated with the acid and pepsin. At this point, some amino acids and alcohol are being absorbed, but the stomach is only responsible for 10% of total nutrient absorption from the food you consume. For the food to move into the small intestine, the **pyloric sphincter** regulates its passage from the stomach to the small intestine. On average, food spends anywhere from two to four hours in your stomach—this can vary based upon when you last ate, if you go to sleep directly after eating, stress, and other factors such as genetics.

YOUR SMALL INTESTINE AND ITS FRIENDS

Once the food passes into the small intestine, the majority of digestion and absorption starts to occur. The **small intestine** is not actually small in length (average length is 10'), but it is small in diameter (average diameter is 1"). It is a tube whose surface is made of very small folds called **villi**; within the folds of the villi are even smaller ones called **microvilli**. Think of the surface of the small intestine tube as being crimped like the paper that surrounds a cupcake or muffin. The purpose or value of this is that it increases the surface for the new enzymes to coat and for a greater surface area to absorb the small nutrients.

The small intestine doesn't stand alone; accessory organs assist and make the conditions ideal for the small intestine to be successful at doing its job. One of them is your **pancreas**. Because the food coming from your stomach is very acidic, your cells would burn up if something wasn't done to correct this condition. The pancreas has a tall order; it must create a neutralizing substance called a buffer to bring the acidic food to a normal pH, which is crucial for the new enzymes to work. Then, your pancreas is responsible for producing all the enzymes to break down the macromolecules. These enzymes fall into generic categories (proteases, lipases, and carbohydrases) but, in reality, most enzymes can only digest a few types and, sometimes, even just one specific substance. A good example is lactase, which is an enzyme that breaks down the milk sugar lactose and only lactose. The proteases digest proteins by making the long amino acid chains into smaller chains that are only two or three amino acids long or even down to just an individual amino acid. The lipases digest fats by breaking down triglycerides or phospholipids into individual fats (fatty acids), and carbohydrases digest polysaccharides such as starch and glycogen into glucose. At this point, we should mention that not everything needs to be digested; if the substance is small, such as a monomer (glucose or amino acids), or it is hydrophobic such fats or cholesterol, it can make its way across the cell membrane and get to work.

 CHEW ON THIS 4.4 You can live without your gallbladder, but doctors recommend that you reduce the amount of fats you consume.

 EXERCISE YOUR BRAIN 4.4 Explain why the enzymes in the small intestines wouldn't work in an acidic environment, but pepsin does work in that environment.

Liver, Gallbladder, Pancreas and Bile Passage

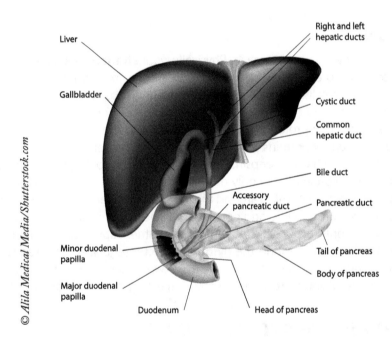

© Alila Medical Media/Shutterstock.com

The other two accessory organs/structures that help out your small intestine are your liver and gallbladder, and these guys have intertwined roles. Your **liver** produces a substance called **bile** and your **gallbladder** stores the bile. Both can deliver the bile into your small intestine, but your gallbladder stores it so that if you eat a very fatty meal, it has a reserve of bile to deliver. Bile is very similar to your laundry detergent and phospholipids! It has one side that is hydrophobic and another side that is hydrophilic. It will attach to the fats in your food that enters the small intestine to pull fats apart from one another. Again, it is important for the enzymes to have access to the substance they are degrading. This will allow the lipases to do their job and break down the fats. The majority of nutrient absorption (80%) occurs in the small intestine. There are two main reasons: chemical and physical. Chemically, this is where the most enzymes are exposed to the food you consume. Physically, it has the most surface area due to the villi and microvilli and has the longest length of exposure time to the nutrients. The length of time will vary just like in the stomach, but on average it takes 10 to 15 hours for food to travel from the start to finish. Just like in the esophagus, peristalsis moves the food slowly down the tube, allowing the food to be coated again with mucus and enzymes before it moves into the large intestine.

 BOIL IT DOWN 4.7 If you are interested in learning more about what substances can stop or prevent diarrhea, search anti-diarrhea drugs.

YOUR LARGE INTESTINE

The **large intestine** is where your body makes its last ditch effort to squeeze the last drop of nutrients out of the food, which at this point doesn't resemble anything you put in your mouth. The large intestine is similar in structure to its smaller sibling, with villi and microvilli. But the tube itself is larger in diameter (2") and shorter in length (2–3'). There are millions of microbes that reside in this area of your digestive tract and have a mutualistic relationship with your body. It's mutualistic because the microbes have a home and get nutrients from the food you consume while you receive important vitamins that help your body absorb minerals during this last exposure to the food. Additionally, the microbes have a vested interest in your body being healthy and not being affected by pathogens. Therefore, they will instruct your body, specifically your immune system, if there is a potential invader in hopes that your body will defend against it and not ruin the microbe's home.

 CHEW ON THIS 4.5 Other areas from your mouth to your anus also have microbes, but in the large intestine they play an extremely vital role in producing and absorbing nutrients as well as aiding your immune system.

Another role the large intestine plays is to reabsorb water from the slush of food that is passing through the tube. All along the digestive tract, your body is producing mucus and releasing water to help in the digestive process, but your body doesn't want to lose this water. Instead, right before the processed food is eliminated, your body will take up as much of the water as possible. This leads to the last function of the large intestine and digestive system: feces production for elimination. The food gets processed throughout your digestive system, but clearly, along the way the food doesn't all get digested. The large intestine is in charge of creating feces, which is any substance that hasn't been digested or absorbed and will be eliminated as poop.

Some of this undigested material is very important, such as fiber. Fiber is any polysaccharide that your body can't process because you don't produce an enzyme that's able to break it down. Fiber is good for several reasons. It will hold onto other carbohydrates that you can digest and absorb as the food moves through both your small and large intestine. The fiber will slowly release these carbs for digestion and absorption over the course of up to 20 hours, which means during this time, your body will feel like it is still being fed. Fiber is large and acts like a big scrub brush. Having all these folds and microfolds in your intestines, things can get stuck. But the fiber can help these substances move through the tract to be eliminated. Fiber also can hold onto other substances such as fats and never let them go. This means that a food containing fiber with fats will likely prevent as much fat absorption as a food with an equivalent amount of fat with no fiber. Now that we have reached the end, let's explore the process of absorption.

 CHEW ON THIS 4.6 The total time food can spend in your digestive tract is about 48 hours.

 EXERCISE YOUR BRAIN 4.5 Given what you know about metabolic reactions, describe the process of ingestion and digestion of a whole organism like an apple. Characterize how all the substances in the apple would be digested.

 EXERCISE YOUR BRAIN 4.6 List each structure of the digestive system and, where applicable, give a chemical and physical function of the structure.

 BOIL IT DOWN 4.8 If you are interested in learning more about pH, search for potential hydrogen.

GET THE SKINNY

Activation Energy—input of energy required for a reaction to occur.

Active Site—reaction area of an enzyme where a substrate binds.

Anabolic Reaction—enzymatic reaction whereby the reactants get together to form a larger substance.

Bile—hydrophobic/hydrophilic substance that attaches to food and pulls apart fats.

Catabolic Reaction—enzymatic reaction that breaks down substrates into smaller ingredients, normally to release energy.

Digestion—process by which your body breaks down large substances to make them manageable for your body to absorb.

Endergonic—an anabolic reaction; it needs extra energy to occur.

Enzyme—a catalytic protein that allows you to function more efficiently.

Epiglottis—trap door in your throat preventing food from going into your trachea.

Esophagus—tube that transports food toward the stomach.

Exergonic—a catabolic reaction; it releases energy from a stored source.

Gallbladder—stores bile and can deliver it when needed.

GMO—a genetically modified organism.

Hydrochloric Acid (HCl)—in stomach; substance that unwinds the three strands that make up a protein so that it can be digested.

Hydrolysis—a reaction that breaks up molecules using water.

Large Intestine—2–3' long and 2" wide tube that makes last effort to extract nutrients from your food and to reabsorb as much water as possible.

Liver—produces bile for digestion and delivers it to the small intestine.

Metabolic Pathway—series of enzymes working one after the other for a final product.

Natural—on a food label, means the food hasn't been highly processed; no synthetic additives, preservatives, sweeteners, oils, stabilizers, emulsifiers or growth hormones.

Organic—on a food label, anything that isn't a GMO, hasn't been treated with pesticides, herbicides, hormones or antibiotics and was raised as it would in nature.

Pancreas—organ that helps digestion by creating a substance to neutralize the acidic foods to make it safe for your cells. Also produces many digestive enzymes that serve many purposes, such as protease and lipase.

Pepsin—enzyme in the stomach that breaks down amino acids.

Peristalsis—wave-like muscular contractions.

Pyloric Sphincter—regulates food movement from stomach to small intestine.

Rate of Reaction—length of time a reaction takes; dependent upon activation energy.

Rugae—folds in your stomach that churn food to aid in its breakdown.

Salivary Amylase—enzyme in your mouth that breaks off glucose that makes up starch.

Small Intestine—10' long, 1" wide tube where majority of digestion and 80% absorption occurs.

Stomach—expandable sac that's responsible for 10% of nutrient absorption.

Substrate—reactants in enzymatic reactions.

Villi—small folds on surface of small intestine that increase the surface area and, thus, potential for absorbing nutrients. **Microvilli** are even smaller folds located within the folds of the villi.

Section 5
YOU'RE GOING TO PUT THAT IN THERE?

Moving and Storing Nutrients

FOOD FOR THOUGHT

The whole purpose of eating and acquiring nutrients from your food is to give each and every cell in your body the substances (proteins, fats, glucose, etc.) that it needs to keep your body functioning. Once the food is digested and broken down, the critical process of absorption occurs. **Absorption**, which simply refers to the process by which nutrients are able to pass into your cells to get to work, can be divided into two categories: passive transport and active transport.

Once the nutrients have been broken down in the digestive tract into ingredients that we can absorb, our cells will allow for safe passage. Think of the digestive tract from your mouth to your anus as a tube filled with fluid that is its own entity. Although it is inside your body, the internal tube is, in effect, external to your body's cells, which means digestion occurs "outside" of your body. Your body must somehow extract those nutrients and bring them "inside," which is not an easy feat. As you know, your cells are protected by the vigilant fatty cell membranes, and these fats only let in limited select substances. Nutrients have to follow the universe's rules of movement; if you think of the act of diffusing the contents of a perfume bottle into the air, you can visualize the natural dispersal of a substance. Or you can visualize they require energy (ATP) to go against these rules and successfully collect their required nutrients.

When we are discussing the movement of nutrients, try to imagine how these substances travel. They are moving from the digestive tract where they were broken up into smaller forms across cell membranes to then get into your bloodstream—our highway system—to be whisked away and either used by other cells or stored for later use. All of these substances are within the solution (fluid) of your digestive tract. A **solution** is made up of a liquid called a **solvent** plus all the stuff within it called **solutes**. Solutes are soluble in the liquid. So solutions can be described by the type of solvent/liquid, the types of solutes, and the amount of those solutes within the solution. For all of life, this liquid is water, and we call solutions that have water as the liquid **aqueous solutions**.

An aqueous solution allows any hydrophilic substance such as salts, sugars, and most proteins to dissolve within it and, therefore, these are soluble in water. Solution can also be described by the amount of solutes that they have within them. This amount is referred to as the **concentration** of the solute. For instance, you can have a 10% solution of salt water, which means that 10% of the weight of the solution is salt and 90% is water. Much of absorption depends on the difference between the solution outside your cells versus what's inside them, and these differences help the movement of nutrients.

BOIL IT DOWN 5.1 If you are interested in solutions, search isotonic, hypertonic, and hypotonic.

THE THREE TYPES OF ABSORPTION: SIMPLE DIFFUSION, FACILITATED DIFFUSION, AND ACTIVE TRANSPORT

The process of absorption involves three methods of movement and each is dependent on key factors. To help visualize the movement of nutrients, try to imagine that we are comparing different compartments: Compartment A is the solution within the digestive tract; compartment B is the solution within your digestive cells; and compartment C is the bloodstream. These compartments almost always have different concentrations of solutes (aka nutrients) because each compartment is selective in what it wants or needs and each is directly affected by the others. This is especially true of compartment C (bloodstream) because it is constantly whisking away the nutrients, therefore depleting them from the digestive cells and causing them to be at low levels in both compartments A and B.

The kind of absorption that will take place is dependent upon the answer to two questions:

1) Can the nutrient move across the membrane on its own (therefore move from compartment A to B without any help)? and

2) Does the movement require the input of energy (therefore, the substance is needed at a level that goes against the natural movement of substances)?

SIMPLE DIFFUSION

If the answer is yes to question 1, then this substance likely moves by simple diffusion. **Simple diffusion** is when a substance moves from an area where it is more concentrated (e.g., the solute is at 90%) to an area where the substance is more scarce (e.g., the solute is at 10%) without the input of energy or any help (moving from compartment A to B without any energy or assistance).

To understand why every nutrient you consume can't be absorbed by simple diffusion, let's roll back to the function of the cell membrane. Think of the cell membrane's fats (the lipid part of the phospholipids) as being bouncers at a hip club. The bouncers, who wear skirts, only let people with skirts come in. But most people standing in line to get into the club are wearing jeans or shorts or pants. Thus, the only nutrients allowed to move via simple diffusion are ones that are "wearing skirts," or, in essence, that look like the bouncers. The fats of your cell membranes are like these bouncers and will only let in other fats or hydrophobic substances. Once in the small intestines, big fats such as the triglycerides you consume, are surrounded by bile and are broken down by lipases into monoglycerides (meaning one fat with a glyceride) and individual fats. Then, these resulting smaller fats, cholesterol and the fat soluble vitamins can move from compartment A through the cell membrane of compartment B without any assistance. Some other very small substance can also sneak by the bouncers. The phospholipids are constantly moving about, and will let some of these smaller substances by because they don't see them. These smaller substances are gases such as carbon dioxide and oxygen gas as well as water.

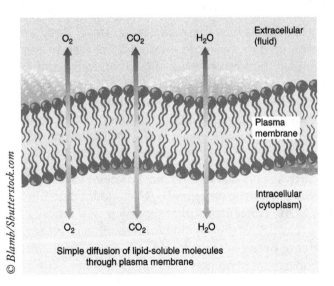

Simple diffusion of lipid-soluble molecules through plasma membrane

© Blamb/Shutterstock.com

FACILITATED DIFFUSION

Clearly, the simple diffusion method of movement is insufficient to allow all of your nutrients (the ones wearing jeans, shorts, or pants!) to move from your digestive tract and into your body. This brings us to the next type of absorption: If the nutrient can't just move across (answers "no" to question 1 of movement), but it doesn't require energy to move (answers "no" to question 2) either, then the nutrient moves by facilitated diffusion. **Facilitated diffusion** occurs when a specialized protein allows a substance to move into the cell according to regular diffusion. For example, if compartment A has a high level of a certain nutrient, and compartment B needs that certain nutrient, compartment B will have the special protein to allow that nutrient to enter. There are two types of proteins that can function as facilitators: Channel proteins literally act as a tunnel so that specific substances can

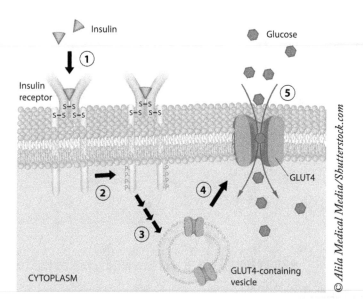

Effect of Insulin on Glucose Uptake

© Alila Medical Media/Shutterstock.com

move through and carrier proteins physically carry the substance across the membrane like a ferry. Just like with enzymes, the channel or carrier proteins are very selective and only allow similar looking substance or just one substance to cross the membrane. The production and presence of these proteins is encoded in your DNA, and many people have mutations that produce bad proteins (they don't work) or no protein at all.

CHEW ON THIS 5.1 Diffusion is the natural movement of substances throughout the universe. As we discussed earlier, the universe wants to be in disorder. Naturally, individual molecules of the same substance will try to be as far apart from one another as possible to reach equilibrium. This doesn't mean the substance stops moving, but, instead, it is equally distributed throughout the compartment.

Water

Water is a special substance because it can sneak past the membrane by simple diffusion or use a special channel protein called an **aquaporin** to enter your cells. Either way, the water is moving from the compartment where it is in high concentration to the compartment where it is in low concentration to reach equilibrium (equal concentration). This is a special form of diffusion called **osmosis**. This can be challenging to wrap your head around because instead of the solute moving, the solvent is moving between compartments. This is really important because dehydration can occur if you consume a substance that consistently exposes your digestive cells to a condition where there is too much solute, such as drinking salt water. If this occurs too frequently, water will move out of your body and into the digestive tract and you will lose water. When you don't have enough water, your cells don't function properly.

Osmosis

Water (solvent)

Osmotic pressure

Concentrated solution

Reverse osmosis

External pressure

Fresh water

Seawater

Semipermeable membrane

© Designua/Shutterstock.com

 BOIL IT DOWN 5.2 If you are interested in the unique qualities of water, search chemical properties of water.

 CHEW ON THIS 5.2 Even though cotton and other plant-based materials are made up of polysaccharides, these are so large and complex that they won't dissolve in water, but make very good towels! They may be insoluble, but they are still hydrophilic and will absorb water from your body.

 CHEW ON THIS 5.3 A dialysis machine mimics the kidneys and uses the same concept of diffusion to remove substances from the bloodstream of an individual who has malfunctioning kidneys. The blood is then returned into the bloodstream cleaned of all of its waste.

ACTIVE TRANSPORT

We have just covered most of the types of absorption that occur in your digestive system. But there is one last type of absorption that occurs mainly in other areas of your body. All cells require certain ions to be in higher concentration on the outside and others to be in high concentration on the inside. This truly goes against the natural order of movement and, therefore, requires a lot of energy and specialized molecules. This last type of transport—known as active transport—is answering "no" to question 1, but "yes" to question 2. Thus far, simple and facilitated diffusion as well as osmosis are considered **passive transport** because no energy from ATP is required. **Active transport**, however, requires a specialized protein that can utilize energy from ATP to move a substance against the normal gradient of diffusion.

 BOIL IT DOWN 5.3 If you are interested in active transport, search substances that are actively transported.

 CHEW ON THIS 5.4 Many students believe that if they sleep on their textbook, osmosis will allow the information to be absorbed into their brain. If that were the case, they would be dehydrated by morning!

Nutrients such as amino acids, monosaccharides, fats, vitamins, minerals, and ions are all moved from compartment A (digestive tract) to compartment B (digestive cells) and into compartment C (bloodstream). Once in your bloodstream, the nutrients will move again via these same methods into the cells that, all along the way around your body in the highway system, need them. You will, however, consume these substances at higher levels than what your body requires at any given moment. At that point, there are two options for dealing with all of these excess substances in your body: excrete them out or store them for later use.

The kidneys and excretory system utilize all methods of movement, and use simple diffusion and facilitated diffusion to get rid of excess water-soluble vitamins as well as excess amino acids, which are converted to urea and subsequently released as urine. Yet at the same time, your body must actively transport water and sugar back into the bloodstream for use or storage. It depends on the nutrient whether or not the body will opt to store it. For the most part, your body chooses to store sugar, fat, and fat soluble vitamins.

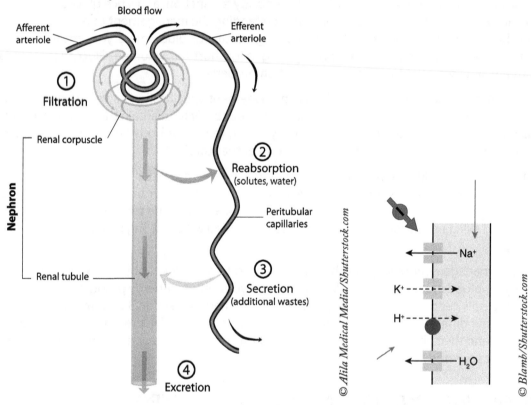

Basic steps in urine formation

© Alila Medical Media/Shutterstock.com

© Blamb/Shutterstock.com

 EXERCISE YOUR BRAIN 5.1 Using numbers in terms of concentration of solute and solvent, explain the scenario of how a solute can move from one compartment to another, which will allow 1) The solute to move via simple diffusion, 2) The solute to move by facilitated diffusion and, 3) The water to move by osmosis. In each description you should describe the characteristics of the membrane, the solutes, and the solvent.

 EXERCISE YOUR BRAIN 5.2 Make a drawing of where nutrients get absorbed, and how they can be used and eliminated.

CHEW ON THIS 5.5 There is soluble fiber and insoluble fiber. Different polysaccharides fall within the category of fiber. Some are small and simple enough that they will dissolve within water whereas others are too large and complex to do so.

BODY PHYSICS AND NUTRIENT STORAGE

There is a term that can be used to encompass many different aspects of you, your body, and how you consume and use food: **body physics**. The term body physics encompasses who you are genetically; how you treat your body through your overall diet; when, how much, and how often you eat; whether you exercise or not; what type and frequency of exercise you perform; your weight; your fat content; and all the other factors in your environment. With so many factors to consider, consolidating these characteristics into one simple term makes it easier to proceed in explaining things like storage and use.

MANAGING GLUCOSE

Energy production is an absolute necessity for your body to function, and since glucose is the main nutrient that allows your body to produce energy, understanding the management of glucose is key to understanding how nutrients are stored. The main storage areas for glucose are your muscle and liver cells where it then gets converted into the form of glycogen for short-term storage. Glucose is essential in your bloodstream at its set point for your cells to function properly.

Nutrient management in general, and glucose management specifically, is a very dynamic sequence of events that is somewhat of a chain reaction that helps your body to maintain the set point. If your glucose level rises above that set point, like it does when you eat, then your body knows through detectors that you need to store the glucose. But this is not the end of the story!

For example, let's say glucose in your bloodstream reaches its max. Your body will signal the storage of glucose, and if the storage version glycogen reaches its max, then your body will transform these sugars into the long-term storage molecule triglyceride (aka fat!). So this is the reason you can limit your diet to just sugar and still gain fat; your body needs to do something with that sugar, and it chooses to change it into fat.

Your body's management of sugars is highly influenced by your body physics. On the technical side, in order for your bloodstream to deliver glucose to either your cells for energy production or to be stored for later use, the cells need a glucose carrier protein (refer to image in Section 3 on **page X** of glucose uptake). There are many different types of glucose carrier proteins that can be present to help glucose get into various cells, and their ability to be present and function are greatly impacted by your genetics and by the way you treat your body. (TBCL)

FATS, FAT-SOLUBLE VITAMINS, AND CHOLESTEROL

The other nutrients that your body works hard to manage and that greatly impact your health are fats, fat-soluble vitamins, and cholesterol. These substances, all hydrophobic, have a special problem compared to all the other nutrients. Once fats, fat-soluble vitamins, and cholesterol move into your digestive cells, they can't just jump into your bloodstream to roam about your body because the bloodstream is hydrophilic. Instead, they gather together in a group (teamwork!) and are coated in a special protein and are herded into a large complex that is hydrophilic on the outside and can now move about your body.

Think back to the bouncer who wears the skirt and all of his friends with skirts...well, now the tables are turned! Visualize that your bloodstream and most of your body is populated by a bunch of people wearing pants, jeans, and shorts. Your bloodstream doesn't want the skirts to hang out because the skirts snubbed them before. But the skirts are smart; they know they can fool the pants, jeans, and shorts by befriending a few of them and tagging along to the area where they aren't really welcome. What this illustrates is that the hydrophobic substances trick the system by surrounding themselves with a bunch of hydrophilic substances—proteins—which are the Trojan horses for the hydrophobic substances. (Don't know your Greek mythology? Search for Trojan horse.)

CHEW ON THIS 5.6 The fat-soluble vitamins get some help from other hydrophobic substances to cross from the intestine into the digestive cells before their transport proteins move them throughout the body.

BLOOD CHOLESTEROL

Fat-soluble vitamins are carried around by their own special transport proteins that deliver them to cells for use. If cells are all supplied and your body has excess fat soluble vitamins, they will be delivered to the liver or adipose tissue for storage. The most important transport proteins, which we commonly call blood cholesterol, are low density lipoprotein (LDL) and high density lipoprotein (HDL). Both LDL and HDL are comprised of four substances—proteins, triglycerides, cholesterol, and phospholipids—which together form what we refer to as a complex. There are other transport proteins that are precursors to the production of both LDL and HDL, but since we are focusing mainly on what your doctors will measure, we won't explore the other forms and will stick to the ones you commonly hear about.

The HDL and LDL complexes are very large transport vehicles and act like a bus for the fats and cholesterol. They can carry fats, phospholipids, triglycerides, and cholesterol-based substances. Although clearly on a different scale, LDL and HDL are transporting these substances in the same context as the delivery of glucose. These substances are constantly in demand and you have a **set point** for each substance, which is highly influenced by your body physics and managed by your liver.

The fats are not just stored in adipose/fat cells; they constantly are being brought into the liver's storage and distribution center and into your skeletal muscles for energy production. LDL is considered the "bad" cholesterol, but it is produced by the liver to help transport fats to the cells for use. During the delivery most of the fats are dropped off from the complex (bus) and can diffuse across the membrane directly into the cell. But the entire complex needs to be moved out of the liver and small intestine when they are formed or they need to enter a cell and this requires a specialized system.

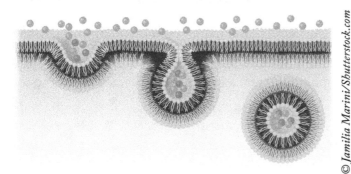

© Jamilia Marini/Shutterstock.com

© UGREEN 3S/Shutterstock.com

When the entire LDL or HDL complex is being transported out of cells, it is much too large and is now coated in a hydrophilic substance that prevents it from passing through the membrane. Therefore, it has to be excreted through a special type of movement called **exocytosis**. "Exo" means to exit and "cytosis" means the cell. These complexes are created in small bubbles within the cell and then that bubble will deliver the substance to the outside directly into the blood. Once in the blood, the complex will be delivered to a cell in need by the cell having docking stations for the complex. These docking stations are called **receptors** and will grab onto and surround the complexes, essentially doing the opposite action of exocytosis by reforming the bubble as they internalize the complex through receptor-mediated **endocytosis**. These internal bubbles will then move the fats and cholesterol to where they are needed. The liver attempts to remove the LDL through this method as it passes by, but problems may arise contributing to high levels of LDL in the bloodstream. The most common reason people have elevated levels of LDL is that they have mutations in their LDL receptors, which prevent endocytosis and leave LDL in the bloodstream. **(TBCL)**

 BOIL IT DOWN 5.4 If you are interested in other substances transported by endocytosis, search pinocytosis, phagocytosis, and receptor-mediated endocytosis.

 EXERCISE YOUR BRAIN 5.3 Explain how receptors are different from carrier and channel proteins.

HDL, considered the "good" blood cholesterol, is produced by the liver and also by your small intestine to eliminate cholesterol from tissues and the bloodstream. Think of the HDL as the housekeeper of your fats and cholesterol; it moves around searching for lingering substances and brings them back to the liver for storage.

 BOIL IT DOWN 5.5 If you are interested in other forms of cholesterol, search chylomicrons, VLDL, and precursors of LDL and HDL.

Most other substances such as the water soluble vitamins, minerals, amino acids and ions will all have a specialized carrier or channel protein that will allow them to enter and be utilized in the cells that need them. Aside from energy production, all cells need to make proteins. Proteins are made by latching together various amino acids. This is a tightly-regulated process dictated by the genes that are turned on in that specific cell. Not all cells are doing the same function, therefore they have a different set of genes that make that cell unique. Protein production occurs pretty much all the time except if the cell is dividing to create another new cell. Now that we see how these nutrient levels may fluctuate due to demand or storage, let's see how we actually use these nutrients.

 EXERCISE YOUR BRAIN 5.4 Your body can use substances right away, store them for later use or get rid of them. There are set levels for every substance in your blood stream or cells: Give an example of one that wasn't covered in this section.

 EXERCISE YOUR BRAIN 5.5 Movement of substances occurs on a small scale and also on a very large scale: Give an example of both a small-scale movement and a large scale movement including the method and the substance.

GET THE SKINNY

Absorption—food is digested and nutrients are absorbed into your cells and used by your body.

Active Transport—kind of movement of substances that requires the help of a protein and extra energy.

Aquaporin—special channel protein that helps water get into the cell.

Aqueous Solution—a liquid solution containing water.

Body Physics—genetic make-up, your dietary and exercise habits, your weight, age, fat content, and environmental factors.

Concentration—the amount of solutes in a solution.

Endocytosis—process of moving larger substances into a cell.

Exocytosis—process of moving a larger substance out of a cell.

Facilitated Diffusion—kind of transport where a substance uses a special protein to carry it across the membrane.

Osmosis—a form of diffusion where the solvent moves between compartments (not the solute).

Passive Transport—simple absorption, where no energy is required for the nutrient to pass into the cell.

Receptors—docking stations used by cells in your bloodstream to receive needed nutrients or signals.

Set Point—the amount/quantity of each nutrient that your body needs to function. Specific to you.

Simple Diffusion—when a substance can move across the membrane without help; it moves from area of high concentration to an area of low concentration.

Section 6
WHAT'S THE DEAL WITH ENERGY DRINKS?

Energy Production and Your Metabolism

HOW YOU PRODUCE ENERGY

FOOD FOR THOUGHT

Every living organism has to be able to make energy in the form of ATP. All of the cells in your body require ATP to function, whether that function is moving your muscles, circulating your blood, helping you breathe, repairing diseased cells, aiding in growth, sending messages in your nervous system or regulating your body's temperature. There are many different strategies to produce energy; some are quick and easy while some are very complex requiring specialized compartments called **mitochondria**.

Energy production can be divided into two distinct categories: **anaerobic** which doesn't need oxygen to produce ATP or **aerobic** which needs oxygen. One major reason that all organisms need ATP is to keep their cells intact.

 CHEW ON THIS 6.1 The universe is expanding and everything would be torn apart if no energy was used to prevent this natural phenomenon.

Your trillions of cells are constantly (24/7) putting demand on your body to get in the materials they need to produce ATP.

Remember, that ATP (tri or three phosphate) donates a phosphate group as it powers your reactions, resulting in the loss of phosphate and becomes ADP (meaning di or two phosphate), which can then even be broken down further into AMP (meaning mono or one **phosphate). Energy production** occurs to add back to those phosphates so that ATP can be created again, which can then go on and power your reactions by donating its newly restored phosphate. Your body requires ATP sources, so these efficient production methods are essential, but ATP is used at varying levels in different tissues depending on the type of activity that is going on in those cells.

We measure the body's energy requirement in terms of **calories**, which are simply the unit of measurement of energy. It's important to understand calories, and how your body uses them to make healthy and balanced food choices. Being mindful of the number of calories you consume will help you maintain a healthy weight and ensure your body is not being overtaxed. The amount of total energy demand for a human body to perform its many functions is referred to as **metabolism**. Your metabolism is a complex collection of thousands of simultaneous reactions within your cells to break down food molecules into the simpler substances that your body needs to function and survive.

 EXERCISE YOUR BRAIN 6.1 Describe all the factors that influence your metabolism and how it can change

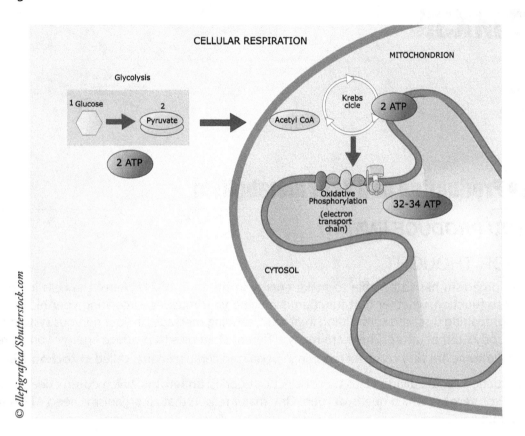

ANAEROBIC ENERGY PRODUCTION

Your body has evolved three main methods for producing the energy molecule ATP. Both the first and second forms of ATP production are anaerobic and remain as background methods to provide a constant supply of ATP to cells. The first is a quick one-step reaction that gets your cells kick started. It involves a substance called **phosphocreatine** (there is that phospho group again!), which is found mainly in your muscle cells at set levels that provide a quick amount of ATP. The "phospho" from the "creatine" gets added on to form ATP, which can then go on to power other reactions your cells need to perform various functions. This form of ATP production is limited, meaning that there is only a certain amount of creatine available to hold onto the phospho. Creatine is a simple compound made from many different amino acids, which you have at high enough levels unless you are malnourished.

Phosphocreatine energy production is found at significant levels in tissues that are consistently working or tissues that require lots of energy all at once. Therefore, your brain, which consumes 20% of your ATP, and your muscle cells, which need quick energy, both require ATP production via phosphocreatine. An example of this is that your muscle cells require a pump of energy when you activate them at the beginning of exercise. It will remain as a background means of energy production and then is tapped into when you have a strenuous task such as climbing a mountain versus just walking/running down a hill. This is one of two methods of producing ATP anaerobically because you don't require oxygen to do this.

The other method of producing ATP anaerobically is a combined process of glycolysis and fermentation. **Glycolysis** is the universal method used by all organisms to produce ATP in a series of enzymatic reactions whereby glucose, a molecule containing six bound carbon atoms, is broken down into two, three-carbon molecules called **pyruvate**. This also produces ATP and another energy carrier similar to NADPH called **NADH**. Just like NADPH, NADH holds onto electrons. If it continues to hold onto the electrons, then glycolysis can't continue. Therefore, your body turns to the process of fermentation to help out.

 CHEW ON THIS 6.2 Because all organisms, even the lowly prokaryotes, can use glycolysis to produce energy, these reactions occur out in the cellular fluid, not in any compartment.

Fermentation is a separate set of reactions to recycle NADH so that it no longer carries the electrons and can be reused by glycolysis. Your body can do this by using pyruvate to produce the substance **lactic acid** as a byproduct of recycling NADH. You've probably heard of lactic acid in relation to the burn of exercising or getting cramps when you run, but it is more likely a combination of the stretching of your muscle cells in addition to the presence of lactic acid that really causes the burn. So, similar to phosphocreatine ATP production, glycolysis will generate ATP at the very beginning of an exercise; however, after only about one or two minutes, aerobic respiration starts to out-produce the anaerobic means of ATP production, except during a strenuous portion or the final portion of an exercise. During these times, your body tries to generate as much energy as possible knowing the task ahead is either the challenging mountain or the finish line.

 CHEW ON THIS 6.3 Your body can recycle lactic acid. The liver absorbs lactic acid and transforms it back to pyruvate that then can enter into the second phase of aerobic cellular respiration.

Other very important organisms related to your food can undergo alcohol fermentation such as bacteria and yeast. During this process, pyruvate is used to recycle NADH again, but instead of lactic acid, carbon dioxide and ethanol (aka alcohol) are produced. The end result for any type of anaerobic cellular respiration is the production of ATP in very quick but limited reactions. Since many prokaryotes are limited because they only produce ATP through these methods, this also limits their size and complexity. Eukaryotes, on the other hand, have evolved a more complex metabolic pathway using a specialized compartment to produce ATP via aerobic cellular respiration.

 BOIL IT DOWN 6.1 If you are interested in exploring fermentation, search for different types of fermentation.

AEROBIC ENERGY PRODUCTION

On to the last way you produce ATP: aerobic cellular respiration, which ultimately occurs when glucose is broken down by oxygen to release energy with carbon dioxide and water being produced as by-products. This process builds off of glycolysis and requires the specialized organelles called the mitochondrion. Mitochondria are the free-floating organelles that act as the digestive system of the cells, keeping them full of energy.

The entire process of aerobic cellular respiration includes three components: **glycolysis, the Krebs cycle, and oxidative phosphorylation**. Remember, the role of many of your vitamins is to help during these reactions of cellular respiration. The first component of the process, glycolysis, produces pyruvate as the end product. **Pyruvate** is then used in next step called the Krebs cycle, which, through a series of reactions, produces electron carriers. These electron carriers are then used in the last step, which is oxidative phosphorylation.

Think about aerobic cellular respiration as ripping apart the carbons from glucose to generate energy in the form of ATP. It does this through a long series of reactions. Glucose has six carbons which, during glycolysis, simply are broken up within the cellular fluid into two, three-carbon molecules. At this initial stage, no carbons have been lost. Next, the pyruvate has to move into the mitochondrion and be prepared before entering the Krebs cycle. During this preparation, the three-carbon pyruvate is broken down into a two-carbon substance called acetyl CoA, a two-carbon molecule, and carbon dioxide. This is the first time you produce carbon dioxide by ripping one of those carbons off of pyruvate. Then, acetyl CoA will enter the Krebs cycle and through a cyclical series of enzymatic reactions, it will be ripped further apart releasing the other carbons as carbon dioxide.

 CHEW ON THIS 6.4 Both the mitochondrion and chloroplast used to be independent prokaryotic cells/species that got consumed by another larger organism who decided not to digest them, and instead, formed a symbiotic relationship with them. Therefore, all your cells have old prokaryotic cells inside of them!

 CHEW ON THIS 6.5 Because the carbon dioxide your body produces during cellular respiration becomes an acid and can be damaging to your body by interrupting the function of your proteins, your body expels it through your respiratory system. The cool thing is that when a cell is working really hard, hence, producing a lot of carbon dioxide, the level of carbon dioxide acts as a signal to your bloodstream to drop off oxygen.

 BOIL IT DOWN 6.2 If you are interested in the evidence for the origin of chloroplast and mitochondrion as prokaryotic cells, search endosymbiotic theory.

So where is the ATP? Well, during glycolysis and the Krebs cycle reactions, there is some ATP produced. But the real bang for your buck in terms of energy production comes in the form of the electron carriers—NADH and a new one, FADH2! NADH is produced during glycolysis, the preparation step, and the Krebs cycle. FADH2 is only produced during the Krebs cycle. In the end, these electrons have to go somewhere and that is where **oxidative phosphorylation** comes into play.

This last step occurs in the mitochondrion and takes the electrons from both NADH and FADH2 and creates electricity (remember the electron transport chain). The result is a phosphate group to be added to the ADP to make ATP. (Hence the "phosphorylation," which is the addition of phosphate onto any substance.)

But what about the "oxidative" part of the equation? Well, the electron that generates the electricity has to go somewhere, so oxygen gas plus another substance called a hydrogen ion combine with the electrons to produce water. This is the very reason you need oxygen and can't survive without it.

WHAT PRODUCES ENERGY?

You are always producing ATP through aerobic cellular respiration, but you start to tap into it at a higher rate when your cells require more ATP. Where phosphocreatine can produce one ATP and glycolysis can produce four ATP, aerobic cellular respiration can produce upwards of 30 ATP! This significant difference highlights how the eukaryotes have been able to evolve much more complicated structures due to their ability to produce so much energy in comparison to prokaryotes, which can only produce ATP through glycolysis. In addition, eukaryotic cells use each method at different levels depending on a combination a factors—the type of cell, the current activity of the cell, and the energy sources in the cell.

The beauty of this system is that not only are there several routes to produce ATP, but also all your major nutrients—carbs, fats and proteins—can all jump into the production line to make ATP through aerobic cellular respiration. Carbs are the only ones that can move from start to finish. Fats can enter into the end of glycolysis and the beginning of the Krebs cycle. Lastly, the building blocks of proteins, amino acids, can hop in at various points from start to finish.

Additionally, we have discussed how excess sugars in your diet are converted to fats; conversely, your fats can be converted back into sugars through the process of **ketosis**. If glycogen levels are low in your body, the process of ketosis kicks in and will tap into your stored fats to transform them into sugars that then can be used in cells to produce energy. Your body knows to use these different nutrients to produce energy based upon metabolic signals.

 BOIL IT DOWN 6.3 If you are interested in how the process of aerobic energy production can be interfered with, search poisons of cellular respiration.

 BOIL IT DOWN 6.4 If you are interested in the substances involved in oxidative phosphorylation, search aerobic cellular respiration.

 CHEW ON THIS 6.6 Different tissues in the body constantly rely on anaerobic cellular respiration, such as your brain, liver, and heart tissues. Your muscles rely on aerobic, but then switch to anaerobic when they are depleted of oxygen.

 EXERCISE YOUR BRAIN 6.2 Aerobic cellular respiration starts off with one glucose molecule; draw a figure describing how/when all six carbons are released as CO2.

 EXERCISE YOUR BRAIN 6.3 Describe each of the three methods you use to produce ATP. What are the differences and similarities among the methods?

WHAT IS KETOSIS?

Ketosis is a normal metabolic state that occurs within your cells. If your body does not have enough carbohydrates to convert into energy, it instead uses fat stores to produce energy. As your cells break down the fat, it creates fatty acids, which are burned off in the liver by a process called beta-oxidation. The result of this process is ketones, which are used as fuel by your muscles and brain. Humans evolved the ability to develop ketones so that we could survive for prolonged periods of time without glucose (which produces energy, which keeps you alive).

If you are eating a very low-carb diet, after a few days your body will respond to the need to use fat to produce energy. The state of ketosis refers to a sustained state of fat conversion to restore blood glucose levels.

CALORIES

Nutrition Facts

Serving Size 1 cup (110g)
Servings Per Container About 6

Amount Per Serving

Calories 250	Calories from Fat 30

	% Daily Value*
Total Fat 7g	**11%**
Saturated Fat 3g	**16%**
Trans Fat 0g	
Cholesterol 4mg	**2%**
Sodium 300mg	**13%**
Total Carbohydrate 30g	**10%**
Dietary Fiber 3g	**14%**
Sugars 2g	
Protein 5g	
Vitamin A	7%
Vitamin C	15%
Calcium	20%
Iron	32%

* Percent Daily Values are based on a 2,000 calorie diet. Your daily value may be higher or lower depending on your calorie needs.

		Calories:	2,000	2,500
Total Fat	Less than		55g	75g
Saturated Fat	Less than		10g	12g
Cholesterol	Less than		1,500mg	1,700mg
Total Carbohydrate			250mg	300mg
Dietary Fiber			22mg	31mg

© *jamie cross/Shutterstock.com*

Nutrition Facts

6 servings per container

Serving Size   1 cup (110g)

Amount per 1 cup

Calories 250

% DV*		
11%	**Total Fat** 7g	
16%	**Saturated Fat** 3g	
	Trans Fat 0g	
2%	**Cholesterol** 4mg	
13%	**Sodium** 300mg	
10%	**Total Carbs** 30g	
14%	**Dietary Fiber** 3g	
	Sugars 2g	
	Added Sugars 0g	
	Protein 5g	
7%	Vitamin A 1mcg	
15%	Vitamin C 2mcg	
20%	Calcium 4mg	
32%	Iron 5mg	

* Percent Daily Values are based on a 2,000 calorie diet. Your daily value may be higher or lower depending on your calorie needs.

		Calories:	2,000	2,500
Total Fat	Less than		55g	75g
Saturated Fat	Less than		10g	12g
Cholesterol	Less than		1,500mg	1,700mg
Total Carbohydrate			250mg	300mg
Dietary Fiber			22mg	31mg

Carbohydrates, fats, and proteins are all used during the steps of anaerobic and/or aerobic cellular respiration. The energy generated from these substances, however, is not all equal. They each produce different amounts of energy per gram, which can be measured as a gauge of heat. A **calorie** is the amount of heat needed to raise one **gram of water one degree Celsius**.

Remember, your body is working on 1,000 times this calorie level (on the Calorie level). Either way, these are merely units of measuring the energy within the food. How do food companies determine the number of calories in your food? It's pretty cool; the measurement is done by burning the food within a combustion chamber (aka a bomb chamber) called a **calorimeter**. As the material from the food burns, it will increase the heat energy in the water in the surrounding chamber. The temperature change allows food companies and the government to confirm how many calories are within any given food product. The carbohydrates and proteins both produce around the same amount of energy: approximately four calories per gram. Fats, on the other hand, generate nine calories per gram. The last major substance that can contribute to caloric intake is alcohol, which produces seven calories per gram.

 CHEW ON THIS 6.7 Alcohol interrupts the normal signal (antidiuretic hormone—ADH) for the kidneys to retain water. Normally, your kidneys actively transport water back into your blood; however, when ADH is prohibited from working, your kidneys stop this process. This is why when you drink alcohol your rate of urination increases.

All food products have the total calories located at the very top of the food label, but remember that this is per serving. When interpreting the number of calories you are consuming, factor in the amount of servings you will eat and multiply the total calories by that serving amount. Then, you must relate this to the big picture. Are you on the course to lose weight, maintain weight, or gain weight? If you are trying to pay attention to these factors, each day you must consider how much activity you perform above your **basal metabolic rate** and how many nutrients you consume that will contribute calories to your body.

On average, humans will burn between 2,000–2,500 calories a day. This is an estimate, and the best person to determine what your limit is, is you. You know your activity, the food you eat, and how your body is changing to those factors; therefore, you can make the changes you need to reach your goal. Along the path to reaching this goal, you may encounter some food-related or nutrient-related health issues. In the next section we'll explore some of the most common ones so that you know the signs and are better equipped to either prevent them or treat them.

Now, we have defined the measure of energy provided by your food and needed by your body as a calorie. So, what is up with products that claim to give you energy? It should be clear that if a product doesn't have calories (aka no fats, carbs, protein, or alcohol) or has very little, then it doesn't give you energy and, therefore, the claim is erroneous!

Calculate how many minutes, hours, or even days a food can provide you with energy:

First, determine how many calories you are burning a day (to estimate use 2,000 for women and 2,500 for men). To be most accurate, a doctor can measure this value (TBCL basal and resting metabolic rate). The quickest and easiest way to do this calculation is to use the averages for women and men then divide that number by 24 hours to give you the per hour energy burning (83 calories/hour and 104 calories/hour).

Next, determine how many total calories you will consume if you ate that food product—ex. 250 calories.

Lastly, divide that number by your energy needs per hour number and it will determine the amount of time the product will give you energy for on a minute, hourly, or daily basis. Thinking more clearly about how much energy you are consuming can translate into you changing the foods you eat.

 BOIL IT DOWN 6.5 If you are interested in finding out more information about calorie measurement, search for calorimeters.

 EXERCISE YOUR BRAIN 6.4 Calculate the number of calories you should consume in a day. Factor in exercise.

 EXERCISE YOUR BRAIN 6.5 Choose a food label from your home. Looking just at the total grams of fats, carbohydrates, and proteins, calculate the total calories for the product. After you have done your tally, check to see if the total calories on the product match what you calculated. If it doesn't, what would explain the difference?

 CHEW ON THIS 6.8 If an energy drink or any food product claims it will give you energy but it has very little or no calories, this is a false claim. Remember calories = energy!

USING ATP: METABOLISM

Metabolism is an umbrella term used to describe all the chemical reactions in an organism. During this complex process, your body is converting everything that you eat and drink into energy to fuel all your body's needs (repair, growth, muscle movement, breathing, circulating blood, thinking, etc.). Your **basal metabolic rate** is all the reactions required by your own body to function without doing anything at all. Think of this as your background rate of metabolism; you need this level just to survive. This is usually tested by your doctor the morning after a 12-hour fast and eight hours of sleep, and it measures the amount of carbon dioxide you expel. Why carbon dioxide? CO_2 is produced as a by-product of breaking down nutrients during cellular respiration and measuring it will tell the doctor how much ATP your body requires to function, which is a pretty accurate gauge of the total reaction requirement for your body.

Your basal metabolic rate accounts for approximately 70% of the calories you burn a day.

Metabolic rate can also be measured at any time of the day without fasting. This type of measurement is called a **resting metabolic rate**, but it isn't measuring the true baseline of what your body needs because all the activity you do throughout the day affects the amount of carbon dioxide you will expel and therefore will affect the background reading.

ATP production occurs at these background levels throughout the day for everyone, but everyone has a different set point. Again, your set point is based upon your body physics. The characteristics influencing the set point determine a programmed range for most health characteristics, including things such as weight, blood sugar, and cholesterol levels. Your daily metabolic rate will increase above the basal metabolic rate based upon two types of activity: either physical activity or the thermal effect of feeding.

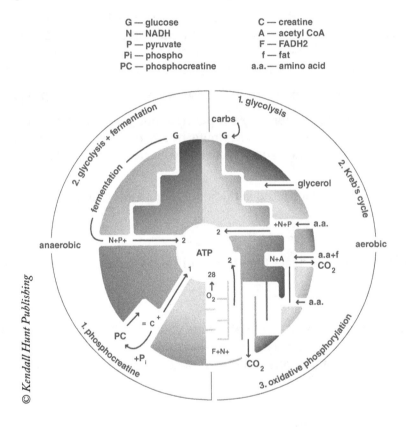

Think of how your cells choose to tap into energy production by how quickly each method can produce ATP. Look at the picture on this page to help you visualize the process in your own cells: Imagine a maze with three entrances that all reach the same goal: energy production. Each method has its benefits and drawbacks. The difference is, that depending on the entrance, the cell will have either 1) a very direct and short route that gives you a little bit of energy or 2) a longer but still easy route that provides four times the amount of energy or 3) a long and difficult route that provides you with 30 times the amount of energy. The beauty of the system is that your cell can use all three entrances at the same time and many mazes exist in every cell; so not only are there three methods of energy production, but they all can occur multiple times within the cell as well.

 EXERCISE YOUR BRAIN 6.6 Describe all the factors that influence your metabolism and how it can change.

USING ATP: PHYSICAL ACTIVITY

Physical activity simply refers to the different ways by which you interact with or move about your environment. Physical activity will increase your heart rate in order to supply the cells that are working during the activity with energy. In a normal situation, your heart rate will increase to a level appropriate to the demand. When you perform a more strenuous activity, your heart rate will creep up to an upper limit around 200 beats per minute. Your heart rate will depend on your physical fitness and genetics. A resting heart rate is around 80 beats per minute. When activity occurs, this rate will increase and will demand increased levels of blood sugar and fat to supply energy to the working cells. At lower heart rates, around 100–140 beats per minute, your body will tap into your fat stores at a higher percentage than your glycogen stores. At a heart rate above the 140 beats per minute, your cells will equally request energy from both the fat and carb storage. These numbers all drop as you age!

 BOIL IT DOWN 6.6 Different exercise routines will tap into different reservoirs of energy. Search for aerobic exercise versus strength building versus fat burning.

 CHEW ON THIS 6.9 Although it seems like it would be better to exercise at a lower heart rate because you burn more fat than sugar, you burn more total energy at the higher heart rate.

USING ATP: THERMAL EFFECT OF FEEDING

The other way you can burn energy is through the **thermal effect of feeding**. That is a fancy way of saying digestion. Specifically, the mechanical and chemical energy expended to digest the food you consume is what burns energy. Not all foods are equal on this front. If a food is whole, meaning it resembles the organism that produced it, it typically is more challenging for your body to break down, and, therefore requires more energy. Overall, on any given day the amount of energy you expend will depend on your basal metabolic rate, your physical activity, and the thermal effect of food.

 CHEW ON THIS 6.10 The thermal effect of feeding for an apple is much higher than a soda because you are burning energy to break apart the apple in your mouth, stomach, and small intestine. The soda, however, is pure sugar and salt, which is simply absorbed. Almost no energy is expended to consume the soda.

Age is an important factor to consider because once your reach maturity around your mid-20s, your metabolism will slow down about every decade by about 2%. Why all the rough estimates? Well, a lot depends on your body physics. Many people mistakenly think that having a high metabolism is always good. Technically, it does allow an individual to more easily maintain a healthy weight, but being good at completing reactions also results in the production of harmful substances called **free radicals**. Research has shown that these free radicals cause a cascade of damage to your cells. Free radicals mutate DNA. These mutations result in cell damage that then can be so severe that the cell will die or cancer will occur. Therefore, high metabolism can result in a shorter lifespan as a result. This exemplifies how the extremes of anything, including metabolism, can be unhealthy. Understanding how your body works and how the food you eat can affect this will help you make the next connection to the amount of calories you need to consume to maintain your weight, to lose weight or to gain weight.

HEALTHY APPROACH TOWARD EATING: FOOD AS FUEL

Although food is a very large part of most every culture, and is the centerpiece for many families, an unhealthy approach to food has infiltrated our society and is resulting in some widespread and complex health, social, and economic issues. Food should be appreciated and enjoyed. But it should also be viewed as *nourishment* for our bodies and *sustenance* for our cells. If we forget that that is the reason we eat, then we make choices that can be less than ideal for our bodies.

Let's look at what influences our approach to our body physics and what can go wrong when things get out of hand. We must start at what we think we should be. Our body image is influenced by how we are raised and what we are taught to value from our friends and family. Whether consciously or subconsciously, the people that you care about the most help to craft how you think about your body initially. But sadly, most people in developed countries like the United States are highly influenced by absolute strangers critiquing their bodies and physique. Various segments of the media and corporations consistently portray images of perfectly sculpted, sleek bodies with very little body fat. That shape body is unattainable for most of the population, and furthermore, we aren't supposed to be the same or look like that. Yet the constant pressure to fit into that square hole persists.

Obesity is a tremendous issue affecting the entire world. There are people who are over-nourished, meaning that they are constantly consuming more calories than they are burning off. This leads to extra deposition of fat which, of course, increases their weight and the likelihood of heart diseases, diabetes, and other health issues. Many people choose to go on a diet to try to attain their idea of a perfect physique.

The word diet used to refer to the food you eat. Now, a diet is the program or approach you take to restrict the food you eat. Every diet program has varying success rates, but the most successful diet programs are those that allow you to be successful on your own and train you to practice sustainable methods. A successful diet is one that you can adhere to for the rest of your life; furthermore, your successful diet is likely unique to you because how your nutrients are regulated by signals called hormones is unique to you. There is no one size fits all.

 EXERCISE YOUR BRAIN 6.7 To be healthy, we all must understand our strengths and areas where there is room for improvement. Talk to your relatives about what family history exists for diabetes, high cholesterol, and high blood pressure.

HORMONES

Hormones are chemical substances produced by your body and used to communicate with your body's systems. They are often specialized proteins that are great signalers that tell your body to take action in a variety of ways. Typically, hormones affect things that you regulate in a more general timeline. Unlike the nervous system, which will enact changes in milliseconds, hormones take minutes, hours, and even days to cause their intended change. You may associate hormones to the male and female reproductive systems, but they do signal other things in your body, including managing nutrient availability.

These processes we've discussed—digestion, cellular respiration, metabolism—are all interconnected; you consume food, your body relays what food has been consumed and, therefore, absorbed, and it then determines when nutrients should be delivered, stored, or eliminated. Your body's cells communicate specific actions, but it's not as simple as just making a signal. Signal production is a key component, but along the road, your system must understand the needs of your body as they change throughout the day, over the course of a year, as you age, or if you are fighting a life-threatening disease.

Along this complex maze of information, you have detectors that are monitoring your body; they relay information to storage areas, which respond by producing hormones to inform your body what is happening. In order for most hormones to function, they must connect to a special protein on the **target cell** membrane called a receptor. Once the hormone and receptor team up, the appropriate change can occur in the cell. This system allows for very precise regulation as the receptor, also a protein, must tell the inside of the cell what is going on. Normally this involves a domino effect in order for the cell to do something. In terms of nutrition, this may mean to store, breakdown, or feel hungry for a specific nutrient. This cascade of information has many players, and this is one reason that understanding weight gain and loss is so complicated. It's based upon your genetics and how all that you do influences your genetics. The best way to understand how to have a healthy relationship with food is to understand how you go about eating is as important as how much you are eating.

PORTION CONTROL

Portion of Hand = Measure		Food	Calories
=	**Fist** 1 cup	Rice, pasta	200
		Fruit	75
		Veggies	40
=	**Palm** 3 ounces	Meat	160
		Fish	160
		Poultry	160
=	**Handful** 1 ounce	Nuts	170
		Rasins	85
=	**Handful x 2** 1 ounce	Chips	150
		Popcorn	120
		Pretzels	100
=	**Thumb** 1 ounce	Peanut butter	170
		Hard cheese	100
=	**Thumb tip** 1 teaspoon	Cooking oil	40
		Mayonnaise, butter	35
		Sugar	15

Another aspect of our relationship to food that can be challenging is portion control. Training yourself to understand how much is enough is really important because humans typically don't eat slowly enough to allow the "satiety hormone" **leptin** to signal the body and effectively alert a person that he or she has eaten enough. Although our culture has changed, our bodies are slow to keep up. People used to have long meals where they gradually ate while they talked at the dinner table. Now, we are picking up fast food and driving while we are eating. This system whereby we shovel the food into our mouths doesn't allow our bodies to say stop.

Additionally, especially in the United States, we have been conditioned to think we deserve a large amount of food on our plates for the price we pay. Our culture has adopted a "more is better" mentality in terms of justifying the cost of eating out. The same rule doesn't usually apply when you eat at home, where you are more likely to store leftovers.

It is essential, therefore, to actually learn how much food you are eating. You must be aware of the calories and other nutrients in all of your food, and understand what an appropriate portion is for you. Although general parameters have been set forth by various entities, each person is unique in his or her specific caloric requirements—yours are different from your parents, your siblings, and your friends. So, remember this is all about you as an individual, so you must embrace your differences!

Now, let's be sure you consider what you eat. **A good rule of thumb:** Whenever possible, choose foods that most resemble the organisms that created them! Having said that, there are a plethora of diet philosophies out there. Different diet programs focus on limiting carbs or fat or calories or protein. Regardless of what program you might attempt to integrate into your lifestyle, one that helps you understand how to pick foods that are well balanced is more likely to work. In other words, a program that encourages you to receive a mixture of nutrients is a wiser choice than one that focuses on one nutrient, for example high protein.

Keep in mind that you need to strive to eat well-balanced foods on your own by preparing your own food. Therefore, eating only shakes or bars and not learning how to prepare real food is only doing you a disservice.

A Handy Guide and Good Rule of Thumb for Portiowns	
A Fist or Cupped Hand	1 cup of chopped vegetables or fruit
Palm of Your Hand (without fingers)	3–4 ounces of protein
Full Outstretched Hand	2 cups of cooked pasta
One Handful	1 ounce of nuts
Two Handfuls	1 ounce of chips, pretzels, small snack crackers
Tip of Your Thumb	1 teaspoon of butter, peanut butter, condiments
Thumb	1 ounce of cheese

As a general guideline, you might consider a healthy *daily* diet that contains the following servings:

Fruits	2 cups
Vegetables	2.5 cups
Grains (pasta, rice, bread)	6 ounces
Protein	5.5 ounces
Dairy	3 cups

Now, back to you being unique. The same diet that works for one person may not necessarily work for you. It is, however, more likely to work for you if it's been successful for a relative. If someone with similar genetics tries a diet and it works, then it is probably a good bet for you. Don't be afraid to try different approaches to your diet and find the one in which your body is happy. When your body is happy, it allows you to be happy!

 EXERCISE YOUR BRAIN 6.8 The three major molecules—carbs, fats, and proteins—can all enter into the reactions of cellular respiration. Make a list of which reactions these all can enter into and determine where alcohol fits into these reactions to provide energy.

GET THE SKINNY

Aerobic—any situation such cellular respiration that uses oxygen.

Anaerobic—any situation such glycolysis that doesn't use oxygen.

Basal Metabolic Rate—all the reactions your body can perform without doing anything at all; measurement taken after fasting and sleep.

Calorie—the amount of heat needed to raise one gram of water one degree Celsius. It is a measurement used to determine how much energy your body requires.

Calorimeter—chamber that measures the calories in a food by burning the food to measure the heat energy.

Fermentation—set of reactions that recycle NADH by taking its electrons.

Glycolysis—universal method used by all organisms to produce ATP. Reaction that breaks down glucose.

Hormones—chemicals in your body used to communicate.

Ketosis—process of transforming stored fat into sugar to use as energy.

Lactic Acid—substance that is result of recycling NADH.

Metabolism—all the reactions within an organism. A complex collection of thousands of simultaneous reactions within your cells to break down food molecules into the simpler substances that your body needs to function and survive.

Mitochondrion—specialized organelles that are digestive system of cells.

Oxidative Phosphorylation—the metabolic pathway produces ATP by transferring electrons in the mitochondria.

Phosphocreatine—substance found mainly in your muscles and is involved in creating energy.

Pyruvate—three-carbon molecules resulting in glycolysis.

Resting Metabolic Rate—the reaction requirement of your body at rest, not as accurate as BMR.

Section 7
WHEN IS FOOD NOT YOUR FRIEND?

Health-Related Food Issues

FOOD FOR THOUGHT

Once nutrients enter the body, a whole range of issues can occur because of bad genes/signaling/exposures. Before you even digest food, and even during the process of digestion, you can encounter health problems. Sometimes these issues might appear to be merely anecdotal, meaning that you don't seek out a medical diagnosis. For instance, you know that when you eat a food product with X ingredient, you get diarrhea. You may be inclined to think it's coincidence or psychosomatic, but the reality is that doesn't matter. If your body and/or mind (which, is, of course, part of your body!) doesn't like it, then eliminate that from your diet. These food irritants are often personal preferences that may present as an uncomfortable outcome, but who cares if people think you are crazy, no one likes diarrhea!

Then, as nutrients from your food are absorbed, your body may have trouble understanding when and where to use, store, or even get rid of those nutrients. These nutrient-related issues are often very complex, based on both your genetics and your body physics, and rear their ugly heads in the form of years of imbalance. When we examine these in the context of specific nutrients, we will then bring you back to looking at your body's synergistic reaction to both mental and nutritional issues and how these can present as different, larger combinations of food-related and nutrient-related health issues.

Let's review the process we are describing: nutrients are digested and absorbed from the digestive tract, delivered to cells that need them, stored in cells when the levels are above the set point, and are extracted when the levels get below the set point. We will start the journey from the very beginning, explaining how your body can have issues with digesting a substance, reacting inappropriately, not communicating well, thinking wrongly, or breaking down cell controls.

 EXERCISE YOUR BRAIN 7.1 Describe what a set point is. Using this definition, explain how temperature can be regulated by burning more fuel (sugar/fat/protein).

GENETICS AND NUTRITION

It's important to understand that your genetic makeup does come into play in relation to your body's use of food and nutrition. Everyone is different because of the unique information contained within many (46 to be exact) molecules of DNA. This information is a simple code. The code is composed of four different units commonly referred to by the first letter of their molecular name: A, T, C, and G. By merely arranging these four different ingredients into very long strings, a unique order of approximately three billion paired units is created, making us who we are!

If only it were that simple. Many people believed that once humans deciphered the code during the Human Genome Project we would know the cause of all diseases; we would understand why we have different personalities; we would be able to see the soul of humans! Thankfully, they were wrong. The code is just one of many levels, albeit a very important level, that contribute to your body's functionality. It is a misconception that everything about you is predetermined by that code. Instead, you have great influence over that code and how it is utilized by our cells through how you treat your body. There are, of course, limitations.

 CHEW ON THIS 7.1 Epigenetics is another layer of your genetic code which determines what combinations of genes are turned on or off normally due to exposures you control such as diet.

Your genetics would clearly adversely affect your system if, for example, there were errors in your code for producing a specific protein such as those involved in food detection (taste bud proteins), digestion (hydrolyzing enzymes), absorption (channel and carrier proteins), transport (lipoproteins), storage (dehydration synthesizing enzymes), and delivery (lipoproteins). Errors in the codes for these proteins could result in your system not functioning correctly, and it could lead to some easy-to-remedy symptoms such as diarrhea or to much more complex outcomes such as anaphylactic shock.

 BOIL IT DOWN 7.1 If you're interested in what causes diarrhea, search for food poisoning, common irritants of the digestive tract, and infections other than food poisoning that cause diarrhea.

FOOD INTOLERANCE

DIGESTION-RELATED HEALTH PROBLEMS

Food-related issues can be very specific and range from easily identifiable to hard to diagnose. As a whole, we don't know exactly how many different types of food intolerances exist, but the good news is that we do know the cause. A **food intolerance** occurs because a person can't make the enzyme that will break down a specific substance. Lactose intolerance is the most documented, probably because it is so clearly identifiable. When you don't produce the enzyme lactase, the sugar lactose will run through the digestive tract and those wonderful microbes will digest it and produce gas. A lactose-intolerant person will drink milk or milk products and get very uncomfortable gas and, most likely, diarrhea. (See Section 4, Small Intestine)

CHEW ON THIS 7.2 What's interesting about lactose intolerance is that the majority of people have the gene that can produce the enzyme; it just gets shut off after they are children. Think about it: Before the domestication of milk-producing animals, humans only drank milk from when they were born until sometime in early childhood. Your body is efficient and so it figures you won't use that enzyme since you won't be drinking milk, so why bother producing it? So, your body ceases production of that enzyme, but you still drink milk…The result is intolerance. Again, stop eating that which causes you diarrhea!

 CHEW ON THIS 7.3 Gluten is a combination of two proteins: gliadin and glutenin. These proteins are found within the endosperm, but are not present in all flour produced from grains. Wheat, rye, barley or any grain produced as a hybrid of these contains gluten.

FOOD ALLERGIES

IMMUNE-RELATED HEALTH PROBLEM

The next two categories of health-related food issues, food allergies and autoimmune diseases, are related to your immune system, but they affect two different parts of the immune system. You can have allergies to a variety of things that are or are not food-related, but the result is basically the same. Your immune system has a specialized way of dealing with potential threats. It will produce a substance called **histamine**, which sets into effect a cascade of reactions. Your body will start producing mucus, parts of your body will swell, your blood vessels will constrict, and your muscles will contract. This is a normal reaction, and the process itself isn't dangerous, but your system can erroneously become very reactive to a particular substance, for example to the proteins in peanuts. You are not automatically allergic to a substance, but at some point—and it can be the first time or, for some reason, the thousandth time you encounter the protein—your immune system will erroneously "learn" that the substance is bad. Your immune system will produce a recognition protein that arms your body so that the very next time you encounter the protein you will cause the histamine cascade. This first step in the process is called **sensitization**. Once sensitized, that histamine reaction can vary widely, from a slight uncomfortable swelling and rash to a highly exaggerated reaction called **anaphylactic shock**, which results in severe constriction of blood vessels and respiratory muscles leading to death if the reaction is not counteracted.

 BOIL IT DOWN 7.2 If you are interested in different treatment options for food allergies, search drugs and treatments for food allergies.

 CHEW ON THIS 7.4 People with peanut allergies are allergic to proteins found in peanuts, therefore they can eat foods that are fried in peanut oil because the proteins are removed. But it is better to be safe than sorry.

 CHEW ON THIS 7.5 The hormone epinephrine counteracts the message of histamine and can be administered to people who are experiencing anaphylactic shock to prevent death.

AUTOIMMUNE RESPONSE

IMMUNE-RELATED HEALTH PROBLEM

CELIAC DISEASE

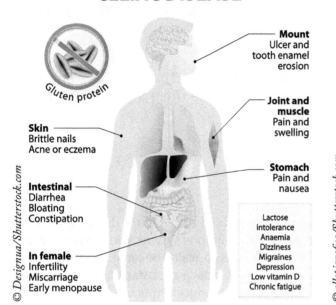

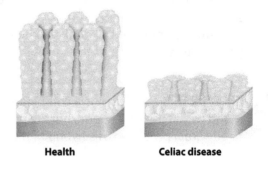

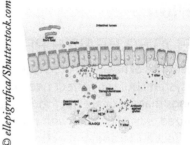

The other immune reaction to foods is an **autoimmune response**. This is where your body's immune cells will mount an attack on your own cells leading to their death. So, essentially the response causes your body to start destroying itself! The good news is that the attack targets a specific type of cell not all cells. For instance, diabetes can be a result of this in that immune cells can mount an attack against the insulin-producing cells in the pancreas and result in their destruction.

Another example is celiac disease. **Celiac** is an autoimmune and digestive condition in which people cannot tolerate gluten because it initiates an autoimmune response which causes damage to the inner lining of the small intestine by killing off cells and prevents it from absorbing nutrients. When gluten—a complex protein found primarily in wheat, rye, and barley—is ingested by someone with celiac, their vigilant immune system, trying to protect them from this "harmful" substance, kicks into gear and can cause irritation, inflammation and long-term damage or even destruction of the small intestine's nutrient absorbing villi.

About 1% of the population has been diagnosed with celiac and approximately 2.5 million Americans are undiagnosed. Scientists do not know what causes celiac; however, we do know it is more prevalent in Caucasians and females. It is linked to genetics, as indicated by the finding that one in 50 with the disease has a relative who also has celiac disease.

While digestive issues are the most common symptoms of celiac, it can have adverse effects on fertility, skin, general feelings of wellness, energy, joints, and muscles, and a host of other issues. Doctors can screen for celiac in many ways, and once diagnosed, the patient must forgo gluten and be vigilant in their eating (and drinking!) habits. Luckily, the food industry has seen the rise of celiac disease and has responded with a slew of gluten-free products. After several months of avoiding gluten, symptoms will decrease and the small intestine will heal. This is a disease that can be managed with a conscientious diet.

 EXERCISE YOUR BRAIN 7.2 Explain how a food irritant, food intolerance, food allergy, and autoimmune disease are different.

HANGRY!

SIGNAL-RELATED HEALTH ISSUES

Everyone has had those moments where they are so hungry that they get angry, also known as being hangry! But how does your body know that you need food? Oddly, your storage cells—meaning your fat cells—monitor how they are being tapped into and can request you to stop eating when they are full. The cells will produce **leptin**, a protein hormone, to signal your brain to stop eating because it has enough stored energy that the body should be tapping into. Your body can also request the opposite action. The digestive tract has a key function in this request; your stomach cells monitor when and how much food you have eaten. The stomach cells will produce **ghrelin**, which tells your body to feel hungry, eat again, and to stop burning stored energy. Your body physics influence the levels that your body produces of these hormones.

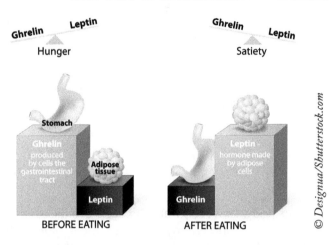

LEPTIN & GHRELIN

Ghrelin — Leptin
Hunger

Ghrelin — Leptin
Satiety

Stomach

Ghrelin produced by cells the gastrointestinal tract

Adipose tissue

Leptin

BEFORE EATING

Leptin - hormone made by adipose cells

Ghrelin

AFTER EATING

© *Designua/Shutterstock.com*

Just like other protein hormones, these signals must dock onto receptors. A common health issue occurs when an individual has a mutation within the leptin receptors that prevents his or her brain from knowing to stop eating. Instead, they feel hungry all the time and, therefore, will eat to excess because they lack the correct receptor. Just replacing leptin won't cure the problem because these signals require the signal leptin, *and* the receptor for leptin, *and* all the substances within the pathway to make the change in your desire to eat. In other words, in these two signals alone there are many possible different mutations in, for example, the leptin, ghrelin, their receptors, or any downstream signals that may result in your system mistaking what is actually happening, leading to either overeating or even undereating.

EXERCISE YOUR BRAIN 7.3 In this section, a new type of receptor is mentioned with regard to its role in signaling; describe how this receptor is different from the receptors that are used in receptor-mediated endocytosis.

EXERCISE YOUR BRAIN 7.4 Create a diagram which explains how your body knows when to eat or when to stop eating.

DIABETES

STORAGE AND USE-RELATED HEALTH ISSUES

The medical world has identified three main types of diabetes: diabetes 1, diabetes 2, and gestational diabetes. The two most prevalent are types 1 and 2. **Type 1 diabetes** was once called juvenile diabetes because it was most commonly found in children. This type of diabetes occurs when the pancreatic cells that produce insulin die and therefore can't produce the essential signal to store glucose. Let's examine this issue as a whole. Normally when you eat, your body will absorb the sugar and once your threshold for sugar is reached in the bloodstream, will then store it in the form of glycogen. Your body knows to do this because your detectors tell the pancreas to secrete insulin, which in turn relays the message to both your muscle and liver cells to take up the glucose and make the glycogen. Insulin also assists amino acids

HOW DOES INSULIN WORK?

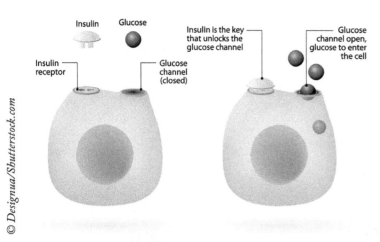

© Designua/Shutterstock.com

in entering cells, to stop fat metabolism and, if necessary, to store fat. Those functions add up to a lot of responsibility, but the main thing to understand about insulin is this: After eating—No insulin = no sugar storage = high blood sugar/glucose! Your kidneys are responsible for filtering waste out of the bloodstream, and when your sugar levels are too high, the kidneys have to work extra hard and, over time, this extra demand can damage them.

In normal circumstances, as the kidneys filter your blood, they try to retain key nutrients, including water and glucose. Blood going into your kidneys contains glucose because the cells in your kidneys need it.

Your body, however, wants to keep the glucose, so the kidneys, again under normal circumstance, are constantly using energy to actively move glucose from the urine they are creating back into your bloodstream. If your bloodstream can't store the glucose, then your kidneys must get rid of this key nutrient. That goes against its natural/normal duty and, therefore, causes the excretory system to be out of whack.

Your kidneys excreted the sugar in your urine to bring the blood sugar level back to normal, but what happens in between meals when blood sugar gets low? Normally, your body will tap into the stored glucose by sending those trusty detectors to tell a different set of pancreatic cells to produce a different signal called **glucagon**. Glucagon goes to the storage cells and tells them to start breaking down the glycogen into glucose and then to release it into the bloodstream to bring the blood sugar level back up to the set point. But if you have type 1 diabetes, then there is no storage, and once blood sugar gets low, your body can go into what is called diabetic shock or **hypoglycemia.** Your body starts to prioritize what will get energy because there is such a low amount of sugar in your system. You will start to think and talk unclearly, and many people get violent and irrational, almost as if they are drunk. At this point, your body's sole mission is to get sugar to your heart and everything else is essentially irrelevant. This can be fixed by giving someone a fast source of sugar, such as juice. The simple sugars will be absorbed directly so it can be brought into the bloodstream quickly to bring the blood sugar level back to its normal range.

 EXERCISE YOUR BRAIN 7.5 Both high and low blood sugars are dangerous, but in the short term, hypoglycemia is much more dangerous. Explain why.

 BOIL IT DOWN 7.3 If you are interested in the sources of insulin, search drug production of insulin.

Scientists believe that the main cause for type 1 is genetics, but there may be other reasons for why this condition occurs and the timing of its onset. Individuals with type 1 diabetes are considered to be insulin dependent, meaning they require an alternate source of insulin. Insulin used to be available only through an injection, but now it can be administered through a pump that can be permanently installed in the diabetic person. Diabetics must constantly monitor their blood sugar and manage their diets in relation to how much insulin they've administered. Therefore, people with diabetes must always—every day, every meal—vigilantly keep track of what they consume and how much activity they have had throughout the day.

How are type 1 and type 2 diabetes different? **Type 2 Diabetes** is often referred to as "insulin resistant" diabetes because the body does produce insulin, but is unable to use it properly. The pancreas might produce the signal insulin at insufficient levels or the storage cells aren't listening to its message to store the glucose. Type 2 diabetics can store some glucose so the effects are not as potentially life threatening as type 1. Scientists believe the major cause of type 2 diabetes is diet and body physics, which means it's largely preventable and can be managed by changing one's body physics. Some people do require or choose to manage this type of diabetes through medication.

REGULATING YOUR CHOLESTEROL

STORAGE-RELATED HEALTH PROBLEM

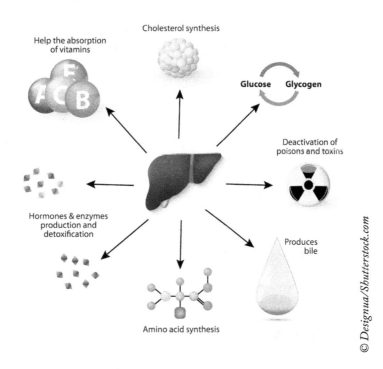

As you know, you need cholesterol to continue building healthy cells, and your liver produces the amount your body needs. You do, however consume cholesterol in your diet, mainly through animal sources. High levels of cholesterol in your blood can lead to a host of health issues. It manifests as a waxy substance in your bloodstream, and can build up causing your arteries to become too narrow or even blocked. If your arteries are clogged with cholesterol, not enough oxygen-rich blood can reach your heart or brain, which results in a heart attack or stroke.

 CHEW ON THIS 7.6 More than 80% of heart attacks are caused by blockage of the arteries of the heart.

People often get confused between the nutrient cholesterol (on your food label) and the blood cholesterol measured at your doctor's office. The **blood cholesterol test** at your doctor's office measures four different things: your total cholesterol level; the level of "bad" low density lipoproteins (LDL); the level of "good" high density lipoproteins (HDL); and the level of triglycerides in your blood. You can look at the numbers for each individually, however, research suggests that it is the ratio of the LDL to HDL that truly matters the most.

We measure cholesterol as milligrams (mg) of cholesterol per deciliter (dL) of blood. In general, your total blood cholesterol should be 200 mg/dL or less; your LDL should be 100 mg/dL or lower; your HDL should be 60 mg/dL or higher; and your triglycerides should be below 150 mg/dL. As we mentioned, however, the ratio is now thought to be a more accurate gauge of risk. To calculate this, divide your HDL number into your total cholesterol number. If you get a ratio of less than 3.5-to-1, then you are in the optimal zone. A higher ratio means a higher risk of heart disease. (See Section 4, Liver)

If you are a person whose body is regulating cholesterol in a normal way, your liver creates the protein transport complexes LDL and HDL to fake your system out in order to move these hydrophobic substances around. These substances are constantly moved around the body, providing the necessary level of fats and cholesterol to your cells. Levels will increase directly after consuming food containing more of these hydrophobic substances and will decrease in times of starvation. This will result in the fluctuation of storing and depleting the reserves. The major reasons levels of LDL and/or HDL become elevated are poor dietary choices and errors in the receptors for these large complexes. Often LDL that is lingering in the bloodstream and can't be removed will find a way into the walls of the arteries, and since there is more LDL, they will continue to hang out together leading to a larger and larger deposit called a **plaque**. The plaque will protrude into the artery blocking your highway system and putting more demand on the heart to compensate.

Blockage is measured in two ways: the percent of the diameter of the artery blocked and the amount of arteries affected. Plaque is extremely dangerous because the artery can become completely blocked or the plaque can be attacked by the immune system resulting in a blood clot. Either way, blood stops flowing to a portion of the heart tissue. If the tissue isn't receiving blood, it can die, which is what we call a heart attack. Many different drugs are available to reduce LDL levels, such as statins. Additionally, there are treatments for plaque through surgical techniques such as by-passes, stents, and ballooning. But heart attacks don't occur after eating just one cheeseburger; instead they are caused after years of abusing your body physics and ignoring the signs your body gives you. So start young!

 BOIL IT DOWN 7.4 If you are interested in understanding other cholesterol problems, search cholesterol medical issues.

BODY IMAGE AND EATING DISORDERS

NEUROLOGICAL-RELATED HEALTH PROBLEMS

FOOD FOR THOUGHT

There is no perfect weight, shape, or size. A combination of psychological and societal pressures leads to the majority of food-related weight issues, from obesity to anorexia. Think of it in this way: only identical twins have the same DNA, but even by the time they leave their mother's womb, they are already different on every other layer of genetics beyond their DNA. Therefore, the idea of having a mold or a perfect diet appropriate for every person on earth is completely erroneous. Each human's DNA is different, and we should celebrate these differences. No other organism has ever existed that has been made like you. That is pretty cool!

Most people have developed some bad habits when it comes to food. We work a lot, have a lot of extra-curricular activities, and simply don't prioritize the very thing that allows us to survive! Furthermore, we don't celebrate the organisms that contribute to our food. This may sound like a tree-hugging, mushy sentiment, but when you learn what is in your food, you start to make better choices. This disconnect between humans and our food promotes a culture that doesn't properly value the food we eat and also contributes to a host of severe outcomes in the form of eating disorders. For some overweight and obese people, they hide a deep secret of binge eating. Binge eating is when someone uncontrollably eats a large amount of food in one sitting. After the episode, they feel incredible guilt, which often goes hand-in-hand with depression because the bingeing is hard to control; recurrent episodes lead to reinforcement of guilt and depression and so on. The outcome is that they consistently gain weight because they are constantly over-nourished.

Oddly, those who are over-nourished are not necessarily receiving all the nutrients their bodies require. In this case, they would be considered malnourished because, although they consume enough calories, they are lacking some of the essential nutrients such as vitamins or protein in their diet. This can occur when someone tries to get rid of food they've been consumed either by taking over the counter medications such as laxatives or diuretics or by vomiting. This type of eating disorder is called **bulimia nervosa**. The individual eats regular meals often loaded with too many calories or eats normally and then binge eats, usually while alone. Bulimics believe that they are overweight so they have a bad sense of their own body image and, in their mind, they can't stop themselves from eating, but feel very guilty for overindulging. Therefore, they resort to vomiting or drugging to feel better about eating, which of course introduces a whole host of health issues. The binge eating disorder as well as bulimia and/or binge eating are very easy to conceal because the individual will eat normally in public and then eat more in private. Bulimics are extremely hard to identify because they are normal weight or frequently even overweight because their bodies are still receiving enough nutrients so that they're not undernourished. They may, however, be malnourished because many vitamins are not absorbed until later in the digestive tract.

The majority of people who are malnourished are those who are also undernourished because of limited access to food or because of an eating disorder. Undernourishment happens when not enough calories are consumed to fuel the body; by definition, you have to be malnourished if you are undernourished. **Anorexia nervosa** occurs when an individual strictly limits his/her consumption of food in a compulsive manner. Those with anorexia think they are overweight and have a very warped concept of how large their body actually is. This type of disorder is much easier to identify because dramatic weight loss due to clear undernourishment is visible. All eating disorders have a mental aspect, but there are varying levels to which an individual will participate in the habit, whether it be bingeing, severely limiting food, or vomiting. Normally, once the behavior starts, the individual's behavior will progress further unless some type of intervention occurs.

 EXERCISE YOUR BRAIN 7.6 Research an eating disorder that wasn't discussed and explain the typical cause of the disorder, how it manifests, and what the treatment options are.

CANCER

GENETIC-RELATED HEALTH ISSUE

Cancer occurs when your body produces abnormal cells that divide uncontrollably and damage the healthy cells and tissue around them. It is often caused by a combination of factors including genetics and environmental factors (which includes your nutrition and body physics). Given that cancer is so prevalent and so deadly, it behooves you to know if you are contributing to your risk of getting cancer by inadvertently consuming products produced with carcinogens. A **carcinogen** is any substance that has been correlated with the production of cells that divide uncontrollably.

In normal conditions, your cells, which are dividing as you are reading this sentence, have signals called **proto-oncogenes** requesting them to start the process of dividing to produce new cells, so the cell shuts down its normal function and takes on the task of producing new cells. As the cell is focusing on the very lengthy process of making new cells, there are checkpoints to verify that everything is good and there aren't any errors. This regulation is done by a set of genes called **tumor suppressor genes**. If the tumor suppressor genes detect any errors in the DNA, energy supply, or in the amount of other material needed, then they will either fix the errors and continue on with cell production or tell the cell to die (so it cannot produce abnormal cells, i.e. cancerous).

Cancer occurs because the proto-oncogenes get mutated into oncogenes causing the signal to be turned on all the time. After this first step, failure within the tumor suppressor genes prevents them from stopping the cells from dividing, and therefore the abnormal cells divide and form a mass (aka **tumor**). Technically, this isn't necessarily true cancer at this point; if the cells remain in the area of origin, then it is considered a **benign** tumor. Benign tumors are not necessarily dangerous unless they grow too large and affect the function of other organs. Benign tumors can request blood vessels to help feed it, thereby tricking your body into allowing it to become larger. **Angiogenesis** is the production of new blood vessels, and this enables a benign tumor to become mobile, which is called metastasis. Benign tumor cells can move through the lymphatic system or the blood vessels, but whichever way it moves, it is now possible for it to infiltrate other tissues. At this point, it is a **malignant tumor** and is considered true cancer. The spread or **metastasis** of tumor cells depends on the type of cell it originated in and the types of genes mutated in the tumor cells.

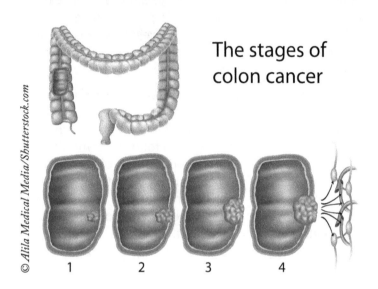

The stages of colon cancer

© Alila Medical Media/Shutterstock.com

1   2   3   4

Many digestive cancers, such as colon, stomach, and pancreatic cancers, have been increasing in our population. There is some speculation and sufficient cause to assert that it may be due to the types of food we are consuming and that there is less frequency of these cancers in people who live a healthier lifestyle. Extensive research has been conducted to understand what carcinogens occur naturally in our food, and what carcinogens are knowingly added into our food sources during production or preparation. We know, for example, that eating meats or vegetables in the broccoli family that have been charred or burnt increases your chance of getting cancer.

 BOIL IT DOWN 7.5 If you are interested in understanding what carcinogens are in your food, search carcinogens in common foods.

Therefore, with all of this knowledge of your food, where it comes from, how it works, and why you need it at all, you have the tools to make those wise choices to create habits to have a healthy life, to splurge every once in awhile on something indulgent, and to have a long life because of your food! You're in control now, good luck.

 CHEW ON THIS 7.7 People who are malnourished because they don't have access to enough food will often exhibit distended abdomens because the microbes in their digestive tracts are producing lots of gas from whatever food they are able to consume.

 EXERCISE YOUR BRAIN 7.7 Describe how a benign tumor can become a malignant tumor.

 EXERCISE YOUR BRAIN 7.8 Compare and contrast the progression of cancer in lung cancer, breast cancer, colon cancer, and leukemia. Use the four stages to describe the different physical milestones for each. Then, list one challenge to the diagnosis of each.

GET THE SKINNY

Anaphylactic Shock—exaggerated and dangerous response of your body to perceived threats.

Angiogenesis—getting blood vessels to supply nutrients enables tumors to grow.

Anorexia—eating disorder in which an individual intentionally undernourishes his/her body and is therefore malnourished.

Autoimmune Response—immune cells attack a substance.

Benign Tumor—mass of abnormal cells that isn't still dividing.

Blood Cholesterol Test—measures LDL, HDL, and triglycerides in the blood.

Bulimia Nervosa—eating disorder where individual eats excessively and intentionally vomits or uses laxatives or diuretics to excrete the food leaving them malnourished.

Cancer—abnormal cells that divide uncontrollably.

Carcinogen—substance correlated to cancer.

Diabetes Type 1—aka "insulin dependent" because pancreas cannot produce insulin and therefore, cannot store glucose.

Diabetes Type 2—aka "insulin resistant" because pancreas produces insulin, but it isn't used properly.

Food Allergy—occurs when an individual's body rejects and fights a specific substance.

Food Intolerance—occurs when individual cannot make enzyme to break down a specific substance.

Ghrelin—hormone produced by stomach that tells you you're hungry.

Glucagon—hormone that breaks down glycogen into glucose to help regulate blood sugar.

Histamine—chemical produced by the body in response to allergens.

Hypoglycemia—dangerous physical reaction to very low blood sugar levels.

Leptin—the protein hormone that tells you to stop eating.

Malignant Tumor— a mass of abnormal cells that is still dividing and moving.

Metastasis—movement or spread of abnormal cells (indicating cancer).

Plaque—clumps of LDL that can block arteries.

Proto-oncogenes—signal that tells cells to divide.

Sensitization—act of your body becoming sensitive to a specific substance.

Tumor—mass of abnormal cells.

Tumor Suppressor Genes—regulate the DNA in cell division and kill the abnormal ones.

Printed in the USA
CPSIA information can be obtained
at www.ICGtesting.com
JSHW05014229823
47429JS00015B/85